How to Manifest

How to Manifest

Make Your Dreams a Reality in 40 Days

Laura Chung

STERLING ETHOS
New York

STERLING ETHOS
New York

STERLING ETHOS and the distinctive Sterling Ethos logo
are registered trademarks of Sterling Publishing Co., Inc.

ISBN 978-1-4549-4641-0 (hardcover)
ISBN 978-1-4549-4643-4 (e-book)

For information about custom editions, special sales, and premium
purchases, please contact specialsales@unionsquareandco.com.

Printed in Canada

2 4 6 8 10 9 7 5 3 1

unionsquareandco.com

Cover and interior design by Jordan Wannemacher

Image credits:
Shutterstock.com: Mauko: 182; moibalkon: 123; tmn art: cover

This book is dedicated to my parents and my sister Sarah for always believing in me.

Contents

WEEK 6 | DAYS 36–40 Allow for Infinite Possibilities   207

INTRODUCTION

Intention

MY INTENTION FOR THIS BOOK Is to share my knowledge and wisdom with you on how to co-create your dream life with a Higher Power.
You can call this Higher Power a Life Force Energy, the Force, the Universe, God, Goddess, Spirit, or the Divine. It is the energy in all things.

Manifesting is the process of you co-creating your life with a Higher
Power. It is a work of art created by that co-creation: a combination of how
you live and the expression of your love for something that is important to
you. This love could find its shape in a career, a legacy, or some other kind
of purpose. It's the intention that drives you forward every day. When you
offer it to the world, you are giving something that is incredibly important
to you. In exchange, you will receive everything you need—automatically.
That is because giving and receiving are one and the same. It's a fact of
nature. It's a universal law.

This book is about peeling back the layers of yourself. In the search
for acceptance and validation, some of us forget the type of flower we
were meant to bloom into from the seed that was planted when we were
born. In the accumulating amnesia of our day-to-day lives, we might have
decided that it would be best to be daisies, but there are innumerable

types of seeds and innumerable kinds of people that we could become. Those of us who have awakened have realized that being the same limits our infinite potential. Not everyone is meant to become a daisy, and when we let go of that expectation, there is no limit to the unique beauty that we can find in ourselves as we begin to understand our strongest personal motivations.

I offer my own unique perspective on manifestation, one that encompasses both Eastern and Western philosophies. It includes practices and ideas from my studies in psychology, quantum physics, energy healing, the Universal Laws, and astrology to help guide you in co-creating your dream life from a place of wholeness.

Manifestation as a concept has been around for thousands of years through various ancient systems. It has gained popularity through popular books and films such as *The Secret*. With social media being the focal point of how we disseminate and consume information, manifestation gurus, books, mantras, and the like are at the forefront of our culture. So, if there is a plethora of information about manifestation, then why are people still struggling?

I don't want to oversimplify this phenomenon, because there are so many variables at play, but I believe people struggle even after learning about manifestation because this practice is often seen as an individual endeavor in two major ways. First, the kind of manifestation that proliferates on social media is often focused on the ego and the self, as opposed to co-creating with a Higher Power and changing the paradigm we currently live in. Second, it doesn't address the important work of healing our belief in scarcity and our fear of not having enough.

So many of us keep trying to manifest the same things without truly disrupting the world we live in today—without wishing for a world that is truly equitable for all, we are left to struggle for superficial comforts. The kind of manifestation we will learn about together emphasizes abundance as a collective and communal achievement where you create for the whole and not just for self. I hope that in realizing your individual dreams you will be part of creating a generative and abundant ecosystem for all that removes hierarchical structures and emphasizes a world in which everyone has the means to realize their personal visions.

Manifestation is a creative energy, and in order to tap into that energy, you must feel safe and secure, and when you are dealing with these issues, it's extremely difficult to achieve the results you're seeking. To achieve a more holistic view of creation, we will take into account some systemic issues such as intergenerational trauma, colonization, and racism that prevent us from manifesting effectively. I've spoken to hundreds of BIPOC people who feel frustrated and excluded because they haven't figured out how to manifest. I want to talk about intersectionality here, because some aspects of my identity are oppressed and some are privileged. I grew up in an affluent suburb outside of Manhattan and graduated with a master's degree. I am a cisgendered, able-bodied Asian woman. While I've experienced racism and microaggressions my entire life, I still hold privilege. I believe that BIPOC people have been made to believe that we are the minority and that some of our countries are poor. But our cultures are rich, our communities are rich, and our ancestries are rich. Part of this practice includes redefining what wealth, prosperity, and richness mean to us individually and collectively. Even though I won't be able to speak to all the marginalized and disenfranchised groups, I do hope that my book will give those who read this a different perspective on manifestation.

We are manifesting all the time. The question is: Are you creating the life you want to live? This book aims at helping you to shift from a belief in scarcity to one of love and abundance—to heal your perceptions and allow you to see an abundant world, and to believe that you can manifest anything that your soul feels aligned to.

The best part is that you don't have to do this alone. That is why this is a co-creation. You always have access to guidance. When you can step into the receptive and intuitive part of yourself, you will have the ability to tap into the infinite potential that is within you and all around you. You have everything you need within yourself to manifest the life of your dreams for the highest good for all involved.

At this point in our human consciousness, we have access to more information than ever before. We are living during a pivotal time in our evolution when humans and our Mother Earth need healing, which starts at the individual level. When we awaken to our infinite potential and are in alignment with our True North, we create a ripple effect that heals not only ourselves but our ancestral lineages.

This book is for the dreamers, the change-makers, healers, artists, story-tellers, and lovers who believe in a future that is more inclusive, diverse, and abundant for all.

This book is for everyone, including people who look like me and who are first-generation Americans in the United States who come from immigrant parents.

Manifestation is an inside job.

The Universe doesn't give you what you want, it gives you who you are, and sometimes, it takes time until you are ready for it. If it's money you are manifesting, take this time to learn about money and the wealth mindset. More important, take this opportunity to investigate your beliefs surrounding money and any negative feelings you might have about money. If you're manifesting love, take this time while you're "waiting for the one" to build self-confidence and worthiness within yourself first.

Once you manifest something or someone, you'll want to be able to hold on. To do that—to enjoy the good things you've called into your life—it's so important to avoid the pitfalls of self-sabotage. I live by the Hermetic principle of "As within, so without. As above, so below." Hermeticism is a set of religious and spiritual beliefs based on the writings of Hermes Trismegistus. This ancient philosophy claims to predate all religions and is the basis of all religious beliefs. Hermeticism claims that the path to enlightenment is through the harmonization of the elements with the body and mind. Your inner world reflects your outer world, and what we experience at the macro level affects us at the micro level. It's based on the principle of oneness and that nothing is separate.

This is a forty-day journey. In Kundalini yoga, we practice a kriya (a series of postures or practices) for forty days straight to break a habit and form new ones. There are many spiritual references to the significance of forty days. For instance, Christians fast for forty days during Lent. There are many cultures around the world that reference forty days as a significant amount of time for renewal, rebirth, and transformation, as well as seeking spiritual truth. I'm writing this under the beams of a Venus retrograde. Venus is the planet of love, beauty, money, and attraction just to name a few. Venus retrogrades for forty days and forty nights.

You are on a forty-day journey to discover what's been holding you back and what's been blocking the many blessings that are your birthright. The word *wealth* shares its etymological roots with *health* and *well-being*. Health, wealth, and well-being is our natural state, so it's up to us to investigate where the blocks are that prevent us from living in it. This process of investigation is presented in a step-by-step way, but the journey is not linear. For the purposes of time and coherence, I organized it in a linear way, but there's no right or wrong way to manifest. I'm a visual and feeling-based manifester, while you might be more auditory. Some people really manifest through affirmations or scripting. My advice is to try it all and take what works for you, leaving what does not.

Each day, you will read the lesson for the day and do the practice. If you feel called to go deeper, there is a guide for that as well. The intention of this whole journey is to have fun and enjoy the process. My wish for you is that if you get anything out of this book, it will be an ability to shift your beliefs and see your present circumstances in a different way.

We are in the business of healing the past, shaking off limiting perceptions, and getting rid of a belief in scarcity. And together, we'll not only improve your life and your ability to pursue your dreams but also add joy, peace, healing, and abundance to this world. I believe that when more of us feel this way, we'll gain the ability to change the world in new and powerful ways.

Thank you for taking this journey with me, and I'm so excited for what we'll accomplish together!

—LAURA CHUNG

The First Thing to Do

Before you begin, I recommend purchasing a new journal. Think of it as a blank slate. It will be a physical reminder that no matter where you are on your manifestation journey, you are starting right where you are. After you read the content for the day, we will be doing some exercises together. Some of them are journal prompts that might require you to write down your thoughts and feelings. Some of them are more interactive exercises that you can practice and then write about if you choose. These meditations and other activities will help you to integrate each day's lesson. I really encourage you to do each of the exercises because they will help you to embody the concepts you're learning about beyond the intellectual level. Finally, at the end of each day, there is a section called "Go Deeper," which adds some exercises for you to go to the next level of understanding, if you feel called to do that.

Week 1

DAYS 1-7

The Dream

In this first week, you will lay the foundations for successfully manifesting your desires. Who are you? What is your reality? What do you want? What is your vision? And what universal energy will you call upon for assistance? We will cultivate a daily spiritual practice and learn to spot signs from the Universe that will give you guidance as you move forward.

DAY 1
What Are You Manifesting?

*"Every moment is the manifestation of the whole. Life itself is,
therefore, nothing but the continuous moment of the whole."*
—Yamada Koun, *The Gateless Gate*

HELLO, BEAUTIFUL SOUL! Today is Day 1 of our journey to manifesting what you desire. You may be feeling excited and curious about what we are embarking on together. Today, we are laying down the groundwork so that we're both on the same page. I'm going to talk about manifestation, both as a noun and as a verb—a concept and a practice.

To manifest is to bring an idea and/or desire from thought to the physical reality. As defined by Morgan Garza, "Manifesting is using the power of the mind and the energetic frequency of thoughts to invite things, people, jobs, money, love—just about anything you want—into your life."

You are manifesting right now. You are constantly creating your reality with your thoughts, beliefs, and emotions. This concept might be incredibly empowering, but maybe you're reading this like, *WTF, why would I manifest this reality I'm living in now?* Don't fret, my friend: I felt the same way. I felt so discouraged and angry when I learned about this in some of the manifestation courses I've taken and read it in books. But I've finally come to a place where I understand. The goal of this book is not just to manifest, but to consciously manifest—or, as I like to say, co-create the life you want to live. Having awareness that you can consciously create your dream life is the first step to experiencing it.

We are used to believing that if we work hard, we will get the "things" we desire. What if I told you that the Universe doesn't care about what you want, but rather that the Universe gives you who you *believe* you are and what you believe you deserve.

I heard spiritual teacher and author Iyanla Vanzant say that most people believe you must have the resources to do the thing you want to do and then you will *be*. She offers instead that it's *be*, *do*, and *have*. Meaning, you have to become the thing you want in order to attract the thing you are seeking. If you want abundance, you have to vibrate abundance from your cells, your energy, your thoughts and feelings.

The more I deepen my spiritual and self-growth journey and learn more about manifestation, the more I realize it's the art of surrendering, allowing, and having trust. If you are reading this book, you are on the quest to manifest something different for yourself. Something more elevated, "better," something you want. You probably want steps and tricks. And I will help you with that! But I'm going to be up front right away: while everyone has the ability to tap into universal consciousness and co-create their desires, it's going to take doing different things to get different results—like a shift in perspective, healing your subconscious mind, or addressing outdated stories you replay in your mind. As the saying goes, "Nothing changes if nothing changes."

I believe manifesting is all about our beliefs and, by extension, how we were conditioned and brought up to believe certain things. If you were lucky enough to have parents, teachers, and mentors around you who told you that anything is possible and they themselves modeled this behavior, then you are more likely to believe anything is possible. But if you didn't have an influence like that in your life, first you'll need to acknowledge your current mindset, heal the wounds that brought you there, and learn how to cultivate a perspective that will put you in the right space to desire the things that will be the best for your overall well-being. Manifestation requires us to heal and shift our perception of our lives.

Each and every one will be manifesting something different, and individually you will manifest different things throughout different seasons of your life. All those things are valid. Our desires are our soul's clues to what we want and what we are meant for. And while our mind can be a trickster, our heart never lies. Therefore, I believe embodiment work will also be helpful for you in this journey. Embodiment work is exactly what it sounds like: getting into your body to help you to drop out of your head and into your heart space.

I remember very distinctly the year 2002, when I was a college student doing a summer internship at Time Warner. The senior staff brought all the interns to the newly built Time Warner building at Columbus Circle in Midtown Manhattan. We stood there as the group was assembled on the northeast side of the circle, just looking at the building. It was the fanciest thing I had ever seen. I was a sophomore with big dreams. In high school, I did not care about academia, mostly wanting to socialize and have fun, hence my subpar non–Ivy League college grades. I stood there looking at my future dream, and at that moment, I decided to create the life I wanted to live on my terms. I realized that I had to take my studies seriously if I wanted to get closer to that dream. This is when I turned my academic career around and, eventually, I graduated magna cum laude and was inducted into the honor society. I didn't call it manifestation at the time because this was before *The Secret*. I relied heavily on my ability to visualize, believe, and take the steps necessary to get closer. As I stared at that pristine building, I told myself that one day, I was going to live nearby and shop at the Whole Foods (another fancy place), go for runs in Central Park, and make lots of money. I knew it was possible. Now, the thing is, I didn't really think about it every day or even have a vision board. I just knew. I believed. Eight years later, I lived three blocks away, and it all happened. Not exactly how I imagined it would, but I lived in that place, I went for runs in that park, and I shopped for groceries every week in that Whole Foods.

This book isn't just about getting things or acquiring things. It's really about believing in yourself and what's possible for your life, and a lot of that belief will result in interactions with the material world and experiences in it. There's nothing wrong with that. In many spiritual traditions, we are taught to detach from material things and wants, but I believe there is a balance. We have to be able to enjoy our human experience, and at the same time not grip everything so tightly. We have to learn to appreciate the things around us while simultaneously not becoming attached to them.

When we are too attached to our material possessions, we lose the ability to release and let go, which is crucial to knowing the truth of who we are and what we are capable of. There are times in our lives that are so challenging that we can't think of anything but accepting the loss. But, as Jim Carrey famously said, "I think everybody should get rich and famous and do everything they ever dreamed of so they can see that it's not the answer." We may understand this statement logically, but most of us want to get there anyway and see for ourselves. Telling you your wildest dreams aren't actually the answer is not to discourage you, but I did want to offer another perspective on manifestation. Before we dive in, I want you to know that manifestation is more than manifesting money, a big house, cars, and material things. It's having the freedom and ability to change your current circumstances. One of the biggest lies in modern life is that *more* will bring you happiness.

I believe the key to happiness is to feel grateful for your present circumstances but also have a deep knowing that you can change your circumstances at any time with your thoughts, feelings, and your will. As I mentioned in the introduction, manifesting at the macro level is being in alignment with who you really are. At the micro level, people manifest to feel good. When you manifest a goal, a job, money, a car, or a person, it feels good because the thing or person elicits positive emotions within you. These are material manifestations that are attached to a perceived emotion. The object of your desire gives you a momentary serotonin boost, and then you are in a hamster wheel of manifesting. While I'm not saying you shouldn't manifest these things, it will be to your benefit to be in the flow with your life. To understand yourself at the micro and macro level. To be the point of attraction to those things that are meant for you. There is a difference between attracting versus chasing. Magnetizing versus getting. Being in the flow versus forcing. Trusting versus controlling.

When I ask my friends and family, even strangers, "What are you currently manifesting?" most people will say freedom. The freedom to do what they want, when they want, have financial security, and not worry. I believe every human being on Earth has a right to financial resources, education, health, and freedom to do whatever he/she/they want. As the US Constitution puts it, *life, liberty, and the pursuit of happiness*. To understand how to manifest is to know how to harness the creative potential within us to create a life of freedom, where we have the unbridled ability to pursue our own personal happiness—to be able to do what we want, when we want, and dictate the terms of our own lives.

What Have You Manifested?

Write in your journal about some things that you've successfully manifested, whether you realized it or not at the time. Take note of what you thought of while you did it. Did you have a vision board? How quickly did your manifestations come to you? Did they come in the form that you had intended?

Whenever I review the manifestations that I have called into being, the exercise reminds me that I've been able to manifest before. And if I have done it before, I can do it again!

GO DEEPER

What does manifestation mean to you?

DAY 2
It Starts with a Vision

"Visualizing is a mental process governed by the reasoning or conscious mind; visioning is a spiritual process, governed by intuition, or the superconscious mind."
—Florence Scovel Shinn,
The Complete Works of Florence Scovel Shinn

TODAY, WE WILL talk about the power of your vision and how the manifestation process starts. In the coming weeks, we will walk through the steps to bring your vision to life, but today is all about the process of focusing on your visions. This is not the time to limit yourself. Today, I invite you to really go there.

As creative beings, we have the power to envision our lives. If you want or desire something in your life and you don't have it, you can close your eyes and imagine yourself in a different reality. We have the power to dream something better for ourselves with our creative and imaginative minds.

I was a child who grew up in the 1980s and 90s, before social media, and I'm so grateful for that. I came of age during a time when I had to use my imagination to visualize the characters in books. I didn't have the luxury to Google images online and have the images of the characters be presented to me. So when I read the Harry Potter books for the first time (before the movies came out), I could see in my mind's eye what Harry, Hermione, and Ron looked like. I could see what Hogwarts would be like, just in my mind. I created worlds with just my imagination. When I think about that now, it actually amazes me that this was how we processed content.

I remember playing outside all day, building forts and playing pirates and mermaids, which is the reason I believe I have such powerful visualization abilities. Children's imaginations are amazing, and my hope is that a reliance on technological devices and social media isn't taking away from that. But, even though I'm skeptical, I hope the kind of imagery young people find online will help them visualize even more.

Some of us can conjure up a vision through a visualization meditation, a vision board, affirmations, scripting, or even just walking through your dream neighborhood. I say try it all and see what method helps you *feel* it in your body.

My friend and college roommate works for Mercedes-Benz, and she always drives the top-of-the-line cars. One time, I asked to drive her car so that I could experience the feeling of grabbing the steering wheel. I wanted to feel and smell the luxurious leather seat underneath my legs, see the lights and the advanced technology only in luxury cars. I wanted to really feel with all of my senses what it was like to drive a fancy car—to have a visual and a visceral feeling. And while I still don't have a fancy car, for more eco-friendly reasons, it was a feeling I will never forget. After driving her car, I could immediately revisualize myself in that situation.

Sometimes when I really need a boost, I'll go to open houses in my dream neighborhoods or go on a real estate site like Zillow.com, and I'll pretend that I'm looking for my dream home just so I can have that experience and feel the sensations of it in my body. This is an important step. You use visualization to feel what you are imagining. It's a great way to trick your subconscious mind into thinking that what you desire is really happening. More on your subconscious mind later.

In 2007, when I moved home from San Diego after getting my master's in psychology, I had to start paying back my student loans. It was the beginning of a hard time, but I wanted to have dreams to work toward, so I decided to make a vision board. This was the first time I ever created a vision board, and I let my imagination go wild. I went there! I put a photo of a West Village apartment on the board, because since I was a little girl, my dream had been to live in a cute and quaint apartment among artists and poets (which was how I imagined the Village vibe would be). I added a keychain of the Eiffel Tower that a friend had given me from her most recent trip, because it was my dream to go to Paris, too. I wrote myself a check for $100K on that board because I had heard a story about Jim Carrey writing himself a $10 million check at the beginning of his career. If you don't know this story, stop reading this right now and Google videos of Jim Carrey talking to Oprah about how he manifested $10 million by writing himself a check. He would stare at it every day until he got paid out for his role in *The Mask*.

Anyway, back to my story—I added a ton of stuff to the board, including travel photos because I wanted to see more of the world. I'm not saying all of my dreams came true at once, because they didn't, but it all happened eventually. It didn't all happen in the way that I thought it would either, but it did. When my life began moving in the direction of the vision board I had created, I began to truly believe that when you envision something and focus your attention on it, it will all unfold on divine timing. One thing to note, though: I didn't obsess over it. I didn't spend my days asking myself, "Where is it?" and evaluating how much closer each day brought me to the life I wanted. I just knew it would all happen in time—and it did.

So many people I know don't allow themselves to dream big because they don't believe it will happen. They don't believe it's possible for them, which is why I ask, "Well, why not?" You believed as a kid. I know you believed, because children always live in the present moment, and they are able to imagine. As a kid, you probably made castles out of cardboard boxes. Why is it so wrong to aspire to great things right now, even though you don't necessarily know each step you'll take toward making them happen?

This kind of self-limiting is why I believe we have to be wary of social media consumption. Learn to live in your own mind. When we engage excessively with social media, we are constantly fed marketing that reinforces what we think we want and need and drowns out the vision coming from within us. Right now, maybe you have visions and dreams but you don't believe that they'll come to pass. Just remember that having those visions and dreams is the first step—that's how it all starts. Visions come alive when you believe in them and you have the courage to act on them, so tap into what your mind and body are really reaching toward and turn away from what is imposed on you by external messaging.

I want to share this manifestation story with you from Felicia Cocotzin Ruiz, who was a guest on my podcast. She is a kitchen curandera, healer, and author. Her story is a perfect example of the power of a vision coming to life on a vision board. I was pretty floored by how similarly we manifest, because she is also a visual manifester—in other words, the power of a physical representation helps her bring her dreams to life.

Felicia wanted to manifest being on a TV show, because she felt called to be more in the public eye so that she could share her ancestral wisdom. Her intention was and continues to be to help people heal with earth medicines. During one of her meditations, she even received a name: Padma. She went on her computer and googled the name Padma. She recognized Padma Lakshmi, who is an Indian American author, activist, model, and TV host of *Top Chef*. Felicia put a picture of Padma on her desktop, and every day when she opened her computer, she would say, "Hello Padma, I can't wait to meet you." Six months later, a producer from the show *Taste of the Nation* (created by Padma Lakshmi) invited Felicia to be on her show.

Felicia shared that she knew in every cell in her body that she was going to meet Padma and that she was going to be on a TV show. She just didn't know how and when. When she finally met Padma while they were filming, Felicia showed Padma her vision board (which of course included the photo of Padma herself!). All of the things on that vision board eventually came true. Felicia still uses this technique with great success, except now she uses Pinterest and creates digital vision boards, which is a fun and easy process that I like to do myself!

Bring Your Vision to Life

Here are some journal prompts that you can use. Consider incorporating visual representations of your answers into a vision board. Today's Go Deeper exercise has some great tips!

★ What kind of job or career do you want?
★ Do you want to be your own boss?
★ Do you want flexible working hours?
★ What do your days look like?
★ What kind of lifestyle do you want?
★ What do your health and wellness look like?
★ What do your relationships and love look like?
★ What kind of clothes do you wear?
★ How do you feel?
★ Where do you live?

GO DEEPER

Create a Vision Board

MATERIALS YOU WILL NEED: poster board, magazines, scissors, markers, glue and/or tape.

First, set the mood: put on some good music that will put you in the right headspace. You can drink some tea or other good libations. The point of this is to have fun and open up your creativity. You can even host a vision board party. Invite your friends over and create your visions together!

There are so many ways to create a vision board, so do it in whatever way you feel called to. But if you need help getting started, just take the magazines and cut out any images and words that you feel are a part of your vision. You can also write appropriate words on your board. Remember, you are telling the visual story of your manifestations and bringing your visions to life, so anything goes, as long as it resonates with you.

Alternately, you can create a digital vision board and make sure it's accessible on your phone so that you can look at it everywhere you go. I often create both a physical and a digital vision board so that I can check in on my manifestation whenever I feel like it—at home or on the move.

Two apps that are helpful for creating easy digital vision boards are Canva and Pinterest. Canva is for creating collages, and Pinterest is great because it helps you find images online. With Pinterest, you can search for whatever your heart desires. A dream home—yes! An amazing ten-thousand-dollar outfit? Absolutely. Go nuts and collect your images, then arrange them on your Canva collage if you are using that app. Another idea for your digital vision board: set it as your mobile wallpaper so that any time you look at your phone, you'll remember exactly what you're manifesting.

DAY 3
Set Your Intentions

"Every intention sets energy into motion, whether you are conscious of it or not."
—Gary Zukav, *The Seat of the Soul*

YOU HAVE TO KNOW what you want and why. Or, if you're not sure what you want yet, you need to ask yourself how you want to feel. Often, we think we want something, such as a big house or a soulmate, but really what we want is intangible: security, safety, love, comfort, joy. Humans are driven by emotions, which is why we're so susceptible to marketing and advertisements. Marketers will use specific colors, music, and visuals to incite emotions so that we enact behaviors. Have you ever seen a fast food commercial and immediately craved that burger? Have you seen a sponsored wellness ad on your social media feed and felt inspired to pick up a set of weights or drink a smoothie? The emotion those ads stir in you is what you're moved to want: you want to feel enjoyment, health, and energy. You're motivated to buy that smoothie mix because it will make you feel like you're doing something for your body, which will make you feel good.

We set intentions so that all of our attention can be directed at a singular thing. You've probably heard of the famous Tony Robbins quote

"Where your focus goes, your energy flows." Your vision and intention are important forces that motivate you when you are in the thick of it, going through life and feeling pulled away from what you want by mundane things. Your dreams help you remember your greater vision and intention and drive you forward when things get tough. Strong initial intentions will help you refocus when the world takes your attention away from what you're working toward.

We can find the physiological roots of these intentions in a tiny part of the brain stem called the RAS. The RAS, or reticular activating system, is one of the most important parts of the brain because it facilitates the functioning of sensation and attention. Made up of a netlike bundle of neurons that run through the hindbrain, midbrain, and a part of the forebrain called the hypothalamus, the RAS is about the size of your pinkie finger and is located just above the spinal cord and below the thalamus and hypothalamus.

Even though it's so tiny, the RAS has a major effect on the way you think. Basically, it's the reason why you are in the market for a new red car and then, all of a sudden, you see red cars everywhere. It's our mind's way of filtering through billions of pieces of information coming at us and showing us what it feels is most important. Our brains have to filter, comprehend, and organize billions of pieces of information per second, so focusing your attention on what you want to experience versus what you don't will help guide you on the right path. It's kind of like why carriage horses wear blinders: otherwise, they'd be too spooked by the onslaught of stimuli on city streets to stay on a path. Without the RAS, the world would become overwhelming, and it would be virtually impossible to follow a single thought.

You can use the RAS for manifestation by programming your brain to pay attention to what you want to see. By setting an intention and focusing your energy, it's possible to train the RAS to reveal the people, information, and opportunities you're hoping to achieve. Intention setting can sound somewhat mystical, but there's plenty of psychological research behind how well it works to help focus your energy toward a goal.

The Law of Attraction states that like attracts like, and that's psychologically based as well. It's just how our brains work. So, if you can program your brain to notice a red shirt in a crowd of thousands of people, then you can train your mind to focus and attract the things you desire. Back to the example with Jim Carrey. He carried that $10 million check around with him to constantly refocus his brain on what mattered to him and what his goal was: getting parts in movies and making money. The key here is that he wrote the check to himself, so while it wasn't technically real at that moment, when he looked at it repetitively, he was tricking his subconscious mind into thinking that it was.

How you change your reality is by changing your thoughts first. You change your thoughts through repetition. All thoughts are not created equal, and we will talk more about subconscious thoughts later, but for now, you will really need to be clear on your intention and be honest with yourself.

If you want to manifest a soulmate, have you already invested in yourself? Have you worked out your relationship woes? Have you gone out there and taken action steps?

Intention Setting

In your journal, write your intention. You can also say it out loud. Say to yourself, "I want [this thing, person, or goal]" or however you'd like to phrase it. Here's what I usually say: "[The thing I want] is something that is in alignment with my highest timeline." Sometimes, the thing that is meant for us is at the periphery of our understanding, so we call upon a Higher Intelligence to bring to us what is destined for us.

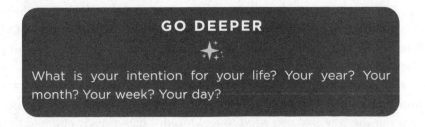

GO DEEPER

What is your intention for your life? Your year? Your month? Your week? Your day?

DAY 4
Connect to a Higher Power

"We undertake certain spiritual practices to achieve alignment
with the creative energy of the universe."
—Julia Cameron, *The Artist's Way*

DOING THE WORK IS NOT EASY. In this section, we are going to be looking at the parts of you that have been abandoned, lost, and repressed. Before we even begin, thank yourself for getting to this point, and acknowledge that it can be difficult—but it is worth it, and you will see the results as you take the next steps to manifest your dreams.

During the darkest times in my life, the one constant I have always had is a connection and relationship to a Higher Power that I personally call God. I've done enough reprogramming to reclaim that word back from my Christian upbringing, but if there is a term that feels right to you, you should feel free to use it. Some people call it Higher Intelligence, Source, or something else. It's up to you to pick a name for that guiding protective power.

Just recently, my mom told me that the only person who loves you unconditionally is God. So according to her, not even your mother can love you the way that you need to feel loved. I had already come to this conclusion myself, but to hear my devout Christian mother say that out loud was a profound turning point in my spiritual journey. I realized that nobody and nothing can fill the void inside of you. Please remember this. Humans are beautiful, chaotic hot messes, and another human cannot complete you—unlike the lie we were sold in *Jerry Maguire*. I had to find wholeness and safety within myself and find security within me. I've manifested some amazing things in my life, but they never filled that void. All of those "things" just made me feel emptier. It was my own self, and my relationship with a Higher Power, that ultimately made me feel whole.

This is a spiritual path, because you are expanding your awareness. As Don Miguel Ruiz writes in *The Four Agreements*, "Awareness is always the first step, because if you are not aware, there is nothing you can change." Humans are gifted with the ability to expand our consciousness through intention, which directly expands our awareness. You can't change what you don't know, right? You have the capacity to think independently of your current circumstances. Let me redefine *think* for you. Your logical and intellectual mind will tell you all the reasons why you're living in a not-so-ideal home, that you need a new job because yours is terrible and soul sucking, that your relationships are somehow lacking, and on and on. If you "think" that way, inevitably you will look around and your observations will reconfirm what your mind is thinking. However, we have the ability to raise our awareness above and beyond our current circumstances through visioning, intentions, and our connection to a Higher Power.

That is why this is all about healing our belief in lack. By doing that, we are shifting our perspective. If your worthiness and happiness are contingent on outward, material things like how much money you have or how big your house is, you will never be full. The material realm is temporal and, quite frankly, an illusion. I want to be clear that it's our right as human beings to enjoy material things, but your happiness should not be attached to material gains, or you will never really fill that void and achieve more than superficial happiness, which can't, by definition, last.

Manifestation is bringing your ideas into physical form. A big component of that is your belief system and your ability to feel abundant—that you can have a limitless number of ideas, and that you will have an unending ability to pursue them. But how do you feel that way when your physical reality is not what you want it to be? When you are broke, have no friends, and are living with the bare minimum? That is why a true understanding of your being is necessary to fully understand who you are as a spiritual being in human form. Your divine birthright is abundance—it's a constant refrain in most major spiritual texts.

But maybe you've heard people say this kind of stuff, and then you look around at your apartment and bank statement and say to yourself, "Seriously? How can I be divinely abundant when I can barely pay my bills?" I believe this kind of response stems from collective programming and economic interests that want to keep us feeling unstable, but it's also our individual beliefs. We will talk more about confronting our own beliefs in the coming weeks, but this is me reminding you that the ability to manifest and be the co-creator of your life is your birthright. It's a power and an ability that everyone has—even if you may not be feeling it yet.

Manifestation is a process of co-creating with the Universe. Being in a 50-50 partnership with a Higher Power is much easier than relying on yourself. Connecting to this Higher Power will not only help you feel the flow of creativity. It will also help you to remember who you really are. When you make this connection, you will realize that you are not only a part of this universal consciousness: you are it. You are an instrument of universal power. It moves through you and can only be expressed by you. At the end of *The Wizard of Oz*, Glinda the Good Witch tells Dorothy that she had the power to travel home the whole time. This is the lesson of every hero's journey: they go off on a great adventure to seek the truth, only to find out that they had the wisdom within them the whole time.

Just assume you can and believe you can. Surround yourself with people who also believe and who have expansive minds, because that is going to make manifesting your dreams a whole lot easier. Cultivate a spiritual practice where you can tap into this infinite energy all day, every day. When we rely on our own abilities, it's very limiting. As individual humans, we can only see so far. A Higher Power has a zoomed-out vision, can experience multiple timelines, and lives simultaneously in many different realities, so we can trust that this force knows what's best for us.

For those of you who don't have a religious affiliation or have no previous spiritual practice, this is a great time to connect to a Higher Power. I usually recommend Mother Earth, the Universe, or Source—all these entities are nondenominational. They are open to your definition. When you are meditating, you will be calling upon this Higher Power for guidance and support. This is the incantation I usually use: *Dear spirit guides, ancient ancestors, angels, and archangels from the highest realms for the good of all involved.*

In many Western understandings of spirituality, God is way out there somewhere, and humans are separate from the Divine. God or Spirit is something that is outside of us. Based on what I've learned through my studies of Eastern spiritual tradition, I believe God is within us and all around us. I believe that God moves through us. This Higher Power uses us as vessels, which is why manifestation should be second nature to us. Our job is to connect to this Higher Power so that divinity can flow through us with right action. It is our innate power to create and destroy, and these are the two sides of the same sword.

Create an Altar

We've learned about the benefits of connecting with a Higher Power when you set yourself up for manifestation. Creating an altar is a wonderful way to give yourself a devoted space to do that, complete with meaningful objects that can amplify your focus and intention.

I have an altar for my ancestors. It's a place where I specifically channel their energies and connect with them. I have photos of both sets of my grandparents, a candle, herbs, feathers, and crystals. I try to incorporate different elements into my altar. I sit in front of it when I meditate and when I do new and full moon rituals.

Your altar is highly personal: it can be a sacred space where you place your crystals, photos of the deities you connect with, or where you meditate. Create and use it in whatever way feels right to you. Connecting to your intuition can help you pick the best spot for your altar. You can also consider facing it in one of the four directions: north, east, south, or west. There are many different traditions that correspond the elements to a direction, so you can research more to find what is aligned for you. I've always placed my altar according to the following correspondences:

North: Air
East: Fire
West: Water
South: Earth

Facing a specific direction is another way to channel energies. When you face north, you are increasing energy. For example, if you want to increase the amount of money that flows to you, you can face north. Conversely, if you want to decrease, face south. Facing east while the sun rises will give your intentions vitality and swiftness. When you face west while the sun sets, your intentions will come in the right timing.

GO DEEPER

Connect to a Higher Power Meditation

Before we begin, take a moment to make sure that you are warm enough and that you are comfortable. Now, close your eyes. Take a long slow, deep breath in, . . . hold it for a moment, and then slowly exhale. Just allow any tension to melt away as you gradually relax more and more deeply with each breath. You are already beginning to drift into a state of deep relaxation.

Continue to breathe slowly and gently. Relax. Now, bring your awareness to the top of your head. Sense or imagine a feeling of relaxation beginning to spread down from the top of your scalp. Let the muscles in your forehead and temples relax. Allow your eyes to relax. Let your cheeks and jaw soften and let go of all tension.

This peaceful feeling flows down your neck and deep into the muscles in your shoulders, soothing them . . . releasing them. Breathe. Allow this peaceful feeling to flow through your arms. Relaxing and soothing . . . all the way to the tips of your fingers. As your body relaxes, your mind relaxes. Your thoughts become weightless, like wisps of clouds on the breeze. The peaceful sensation flows through your chest and your stomach. Feel how this area gently rises and falls as you breathe . . . slowly and deeply. Soothing and relaxing. Turn your attention to your back, and feel this relaxing sensation flow all the way down your spine. Now the peaceful feeling flows through your lower body. Relax your buttocks . . . the back of your thighs . . . the front of your thighs. Feel all these large, strong muscles becoming loose and relaxed. Soothing feelings flow down through your knees, and into your calves. Your ankles relax. Now your feet relax.

Your entire body is soft, calm, and relaxed. Now it's time to leave the external world behind and go on an inner journey. A journey to a place of deep inner stillness.

Feel an expansiveness in your heart space. Imagine a bright golden light emanating out from your heart space. This light extends out in front of you, above you, beneath you, and all around you. This light creates a beautiful aura that protects you. You are safe and protected. Tune in to that energy that is within you and all around you. The energy of unconditional love. A loving presence. Notice if you are in the presence of an angel, ancestor, spirit animal, or guide. At this time, you can just acknowledge them and feel the loving presence within you and all around you. If you feel comfortable and they want to give you a message, you can take this time to receive the message. Establishing a connection to your Higher Power feels like love and an opening up of your heart space. Just focus on your intention and allow the rest to unfold.

Take a moment here to notice any sensations in your body. Ask yourself if you see any images, colors, or signs. When you've connected to this presence long enough, you can bring awareness into your physical body. Stretch your arms up, then wiggle your toes and fingers. Rotate your ankles and wrists. Slowly open your eyes and come back to your space.

DAY 5
Sadhana:
A Daily Spiritual Practice

"Spiritual practice is not just sitting and meditation. Practice is looking, thinking, touching, drinking, eating, and talking. Every act, every breath, and every step can be practice and can help us to become more ourselves."
—Thich Nhat Hanh, *Your True Home*

MANY ANCIENT CULTURES and spiritual philosophies have some type of practice that could be called prayer. Many also incorporate meditation as a spiritual practice, even if it isn't called that. To me, prayer and meditation are times when I get centered and grounded within myself and with my Higher Power. Again, use whatever terms you want for these practices: you can call it a mindfulness practice, intention setting, stillness, or contemplation. Your Higher Power might be the Universe, Goddess, Mother Earth, nature, or the Force, as in *Star Wars*.

Daily devotion is a time when you set an intention to quiet your mind and to notice and be aware of your inner world and the energy around you. This is a time when you can tap into the higher realms of your higher self, accessing your intuition to help guide you. This kind of stillness is something that the ego will take as a major challenge—the first step is getting past its intervention. After all, the psychological definition of *ego* is the identity of the individual self. In Freudian and Jungian psychology, the ego is defined as the center of your awareness and the framework of your individual being. When you have beliefs or ideas about yourself, that is your ego.

You've probably heard someone say, "Wow, they have a really big ego" when that person boasts about themself. This is not the ego that I will be referring to. I am referring to the spiritual ego, which is the part of us that feels separated from our spiritual consciousness. It is the veil that separates us from our universal consciousness. It is our perception of being separate from one another, the Universe, Source, and all things. Most spiritual philosophies point to our attachment to our egos as the cause of human suffering. And that may be a partial truth, but the ego is not a bad thing in and of itself. It is quite necessary for our human experience. Spiritual practices and tools just help us to balance our ego with our spiritual essence, with the ultimate goal of integrating the two.

Connecting to our higher self and this Higher Power helps us remember our intention and vision. It puts us in the right space to let go of what is not in alignment with our vision and embrace who we need to be in order to manifest it. Take the time to get to this place, or if you have never tried it, give yourself some grace and take a shot at it. Listen and allow your heart and mind to open and allow what it is that needs to be birthed through your own consciousness. Create mindful rituals for your manifestation. For example, you could try setting a meditation schedule, drinking some cacao or tea before each intention-setting practice, or pulling some tarot cards for guidance before you settle in.

You might have heard of the 5D, or the fifth dimension, by now, particularly if you're up on the spiritual zeitgeist. Other terms for the 5D are the unified field, unity consciousness, or the one life force energy, which connects us all to infinite possibilities and timelines. In her book *Big Magic*, Elizabeth Gilbert talks about how everyone can tune in to this creative field, but if you don't take action on what you find there, the idea will go to someone else that the Creator believes *will* bring it to life. Gilbert is articulating that there is a 5D, a unified field of all the creative ideas that will ever be and ever were. Every song and every book has already been written, but you need to tap into this creative field to get the download. In order for us to access the 5D, we have to be patient and still, have discernment for what's coming through, and then take action when a thought or an idea comes to us.

In yoga, we commit to a *sadhana*, a daily spiritual practice. By creating a daily meditation practice and rituals, it helps you to connect to a Higher Power so you can access that infinite creative potential. Think of the exercises in this book as the beginning of your sadhana. Unhealthy patterns are broken through repetition. I believe daily rituals are a spiritual pathway to break the habits that no longer serve us and create new ones that support our evolution.

Try an Invocation

This is the invocation I use to open up my prayers and meditations. You can use it until you create your own.

> *I give thanks to the heart of the sky. Thank you to the sun, the moon, the stars, and the planets for creating the energetic shifts that I have been asking for. Thank you to my spirit guides for sending me the signs and synchronicities that lead me on my path. Thank you to the element of air for giving me right perception and mental clarity.*
>
> *I give thanks to the heart of the earth. Thank you to the roots of the trees that help me feel grounded down to earth. Thank you to the ancient ancestors whose blood runs through my veins. Thank you to the keepers of this land, the Lenape people [add*

the appropriate indigenous name here if it applies to where you live]. *Thank you to Mother Earth, Gaia, for all of the abundance and creative energy you nourish me with. Thank you to my plant allies* [you can name them here] *and animal allies for supporting me on my journey.*

I give thanks to the heart of the waters. Thank you for the ebb and flow of life. When there's an ebb, I'm reminded of the abundance within me and the eventual flow of life. Thank you for the waters that purify and cleanse us of what no longer serves us. Thank you to the oceans, lakes, rivers, and streams. Thank you for allowing me to feel more into my emotions and co-create my reality with Spirit.

I give thanks to the heart of the fire. Thank you for the transmutation of what no longer serves me. Thank you for allowing me to burn away the limiting beliefs so that I can rise above my ashes. Thank you for the vision and the passion, the courage to follow my path.

Thank you to all four directions—the north, the south, the east, and the west—my spirit guides and angels from the highest realms for the good of all involved.

Thank you.

GO DEEPER

Create an offering for Mother Earth, your ancestors, deity, God, or Goddess

When I create my offerings, it's very simple: it's more about the intention and the energy that you give versus what you are offering. If it's a specific day like the spring or fall equinoxes or the summer or winter solstices, I will buy special flowers for the occasion. I have a collection now of dried flowers that I save for offerings. On a new or full moon, I will offer the flowers to the earth as a gesture of gratitude. I will also say a little prayer for someone who needs it. We will explore the energetic properties of giving and receiving more on Day 9. We offer something because we are saying thank you for what we have received and what we are about to receive. Your offerings can be anything that is biodegradable.

DAY 6
Signs and Synchronicities

"The simultaneous occurrence of a certain psychic state
with one or more external events which appear
as meaningful parallels to the momentary subjective
state-and, in certain cases, vice-versa."
—C.G. Jung, *Synchronicity*

I DO NOT BELIEVE IN COINCIDENCES. I never have and I never will. However, what I do know is that there's a magical thread that weaves through everything, creating patterns and synchronicities. Noticing these occurrences is something I've always been kind of obsessed with. I believe signs and synchronicities are ways that the other realms communicate with you, and that it's your job to decode them and make sense of what they are trying to tell you. This is essentially mysticism and the occult in a nutshell.

When I tell some people that I was able to get through some of my darkest times with tarot and astrology, they think I'm nuts. But, in 2020 I realized that Spirit was speaking to me through the cards. I've heard this term called *cartomancy*, which is a form of divination. The root word of divination is *divine*. So, put simply, I figured out a way to communicate with Spirit through divination tools. And with the help of journaling, I was able to pinpoint what I needed to focus on at any given time. I believe this because everything carries energy.

Through my training as a Reiki master teacher, I've begun to see everything in this world through an energetic perspective. Because Spirit doesn't speak English, they communicate through numbers and symbols. Whenever I see an 1111, my guides and I have both established that this is them telling me that my thoughts and actions are in alignment with my desires. There are other signs, too. My ancestors like to leave me feathers everywhere. I've built a pretty impressive collection of them. It works the same way: when I see a feather, I know I'm on the right track.

This kind of relationship can extend to other literal signs such as the lyrics of songs, or numbers that seem to be occurring frequently in your life. Pay attention, because you're being led. Sometimes what you'll notice is just a sign of encouragement, but others will lead you to someone you need to meet. For my part, when I look back to these kinds of synchronicities and connecting the dots, I always see how chance meetings led me to opportunities. When these opportunities are presented to you, your job is to take them! When you see a sign, that's when you must act. Western cultures such as in the United States tend to be action oriented, but as you will learn, there is a time to act and a time to rest. This is your day to think about what the difference is: when you should act quickly and decisively, and when you should wait, contemplate, and make yourself open to messages from the Divine. Constant, nonsensical action leads us to burnout. We are human beings, we are not robots, and we must take the time to rest so that we can see what the Universe is trying to send us. So if you are getting signs that it's time to surrender, you should take notice of those, too. You'll avoid the cycle of sickness, injury, and limited perspective that comes with burnout.

You set intentions on Day 3, so by now, you've taken the first step toward connecting to a Higher Power. Now that you've opened yourself up to that connection, you are going to learn how to navigate your way through signs and synchronicities.

As Nikola Tesla said, "If you knew the magnificence of 3, 6, and 9, you would have a key to the universe." During the quarantine of 2020, like so many of us, I got really into TikTok. It was the first time I began sharing my spiritual practices openly and speaking about what I believed in. I was floored by the number of people who responded to these messages: it just showed me that during this period of challenge and conflict, people wanted to believe again.

In 2020, I shared a video about Nikola Tesla's fascination with 3, 6, and 9 as well as the significance of the numerology. The 369 method of manifestation can be found all over TikTok and YouTube. You basically use repetition to either script or say your affirmations three, six, and nine times.

The number 3 represents creativity. It takes two people to create a baby. An egg and a sperm create a zygote. In the tarot, the third card is the Empress, which is a card about creation, fertility, and abundance.

The number 6 is of harmony and balance. It has the qualities of Venus, and in the tarot is the Lovers card, which is about partnerships. Number 6 holds the vibration of unconditional love and matters of the heart.

The number 9 is of completion, but not the end. Think of it as a cycle during which something is being transformed. The 9 is a wise number that can only be gained through lived experiences. The number 9 means that it's time to share that wisdom with others. The ninth card in the tarot is the Hermit, which is ruled by Virgo. The Hermit is about having all the answers within yourself and possessing the ability to connect to the Divine.

Nikola Tesla believed so deeply in the energy of these numbers that he would only stay in hotel rooms that had the numbers 3, 6, or 9. He often repeated behaviors three times. Although the act of repeating a behavior three times might seem simply compulsive, we learn through repetition.

We unlearn through repetition. We rewire our brains through repetition. Doing something three times naturally helps when you are learning new habits, banishing old ones, and teaching yourself to default to this action as opposed to another one.

Have you ever had a dream and you saw your dream play out in your waking life? Have you ever experienced déjà vu? Have you thought of someone and then they called or texted you? You might think these events have nothing to do with each other, but when you send an energetic thought out, it will always come back to you in some form. Similar to what we discussed yesterday about the 5D and the unified field, when you ask for guidance or you ask for a sign, your request doesn't just go out there with nothing happening. Something always comes back to you when you put energy out into the Universe. It's one of the universal laws.

Seeing Signs

Once you've set an intention, make sure to journal and take note of all the signs and synchronicities you notice. It doesn't matter how "crazy" you think they are. If you see a crow or take notice of the time 11:11 on a clock, make sure to take a note! This is especially true if you happen to see repeating patterns. Notice who comes into your energy field. If you see the same person several times and you get an intuitive hit to introduce yourself, do it—because why not?

Some questions you can ask yourself when you see synchronicities are:

* Why did I see this person or receive this information at this moment?
* What was I thinking about during this time?
* How does this fit into my journey? Is it related to my intention?

GO DEEPER

✦

On Day 4, you created an altar to connect to your Higher Power. Sit at your altar, or any other place that is sacred to you, and take some time to connect to this Higher Power and ask them for a sign. Make a note every time you notice the sign in your journal.

DAY 7
Start Where You Are

"Start where you are, use what you have, do what you can."
—Arthur Ashe

BEFORE I BEGIN, the title of this lesson comes with a major caveat. Your "reality" is a collection of so many things, in addition to the dreams and visions you are manifesting. You are not a blank slate into which you call a dream. Your reality includes your present moment: your relationships, your socioeconomic status, your ancestors' stories, your intergenerational trauma. All should be considered, and all should be honored. The fact that you are manifesting your dreams should not discount the healing you are doing or will do, and healing is always encouraged. That said, this is the day to start thinking about the process that happens when you take the dreams you have uncovered through meditation, intention, and communication with your higher self and make them real.

When I look back at my life and remember how I successfully manifested the things I wanted, I try to take note of how I did it: how I felt and what I did. And the thing I remember the most is that I believed my dreams were possible, and I let them go. I had crazy trust and a deep knowing that everything would happen. And while all of us have an easier time manifesting some things as opposed to others, a successful manifestation really boils down to our beliefs. I invite you to examine the feeling you get when you just *know* and apply it to the thing you are manifesting. If you can't imagine it, then it's more of a question of, well, why not? Why don't you believe it's possible?

Some of us may believe in ourselves, but it is more of a challenge to find people who believe in us. Trust me, my Korean parents said we could be anything we imagined until it was time to pick a college. Then all of a sudden it was "You have to pick a major that provides you with financial stability." Growing up, I didn't know exactly what I wanted to be, but I knew I wanted to travel the world, create beautiful art, and meet different kinds of people. Which is what I do now, so this is further confirmation that the soul *always* knows.

In high school, my dream college was the Rhode Island School of Design. I knew that I wanted to do something creative, and art school seemed like the right choice for me. But, listening to my parents' advice as an eighteen-year-old, instead I went to a liberal arts school. I don't regret that decision, because I believe everything happens for a reason. But that one decision to choose safety and security, listening to someone else's thoughts about my life versus my gut, was the first time I would betray myself and my soul. As a result, art dropped out of my life, and in later years I abandoned my creative goals altogether. Part of my healing process now is to create more time and space to create art again.

My parents are baby boomers who grew up in a historical period of scarcity. So, of course, from their perspective, they would prioritize stability and money over dreams and love for what you do. Knowing this, in addition to doing ancestral healing, which was so transformative for me, as it gave me compassion for what they went through. It gave me an understanding that I could be the chain breaker and heal my lineage by choosing something I loved after they had denied themselves. But to do that, I knew I had to completely overhaul my mindset, because traditionally in Korean culture, we have deep filial piety—a reverence for our elders, parents, and ancestors that can lead to placing their expectations above our own dreams.

If what my parents said was true—you can be anything that you want to be—and you hear that same messaging in children's books and movies, then what the heck happened? Why aren't more adults happy and satisfied? It's because our beliefs have been hijacked. We were taught to prioritize safety, security, status, money, and greed over what feels truly aligned with our hearts. What we really loved to do as children can give us some clues about what we love to do as adults. We've lost the connection to our inner child, and therefore, at a certain point in our lives, we stopped imagining and playing. We traded in our dreams in the pursuit to climb up the proverbial corporate ladder.

If you are reading this and you are BIPOC, LGBTQIA+, or categorized as a minority or an "other," all the more power to you, because consciously or unconsciously, by being aware of these things, you are already healing your perceptions. The karmic patterns (if you believe in that kind of thing) stops at *you*.

Our creation of our reality directly impacts the collective and the collective dream.

We shift our reality by the decisions we make on a day-to-day basis because we have free will. We usually resist because our minds are habitual. Humans like routines and habits to create safety. Just knowing that you can choose differently from what you were taught, or the experiences you were limited to, is your ticket to freedom.

What Parts of You Have Been Abandoned?

Take some time to meditate and sit in stillness. Think about your past and try to remember the times that you didn't pursue something that you loved because you were told not to or you weren't encouraged to.

You may have missed an opportunity at some point in your life, but take this moment to give yourself—and anyone who may have pressured you to take a path that was not in alignment with your highest self—some grace. Remember that you may feel that you have abandoned a part of yourself, but you can always recover it if you act with intention. Consider your vision and resolve to move toward opportunities that will help you manifest it in the future. Take a moment to identify a part of yourself that has been neglected and abandoned, and send kindness and attention to that part of your personality.

GO DEEPER

If you feel called to journal more, elaborate on the above. Write down all the times that you can remember that you did something or made a decision about something based on security and safety. When did you choose fear over love?

Week 2

DAYS 8–14

Alignment

The second week of our journey is all about living in alignment with our values. We will learn how to be our truest selves by separating truth and illusion, learning to give and receive, and centering ourselves with self-love. We'll learn the power of joy—living for *now*—and throwing ourselves joyfully into the reality we are co-creating by being present and in sync with the rhythms of nature.

DAY 8
Maya: Recognizing the Illusion

"In the beginning there was faith—which is childish; trust—
which is vain; and illusion—which is dangerous."
—Elie Wiesel, *Night*

YOU'VE MADE IT THROUGH our first week together. I'm so proud of you! During the first week, we laid down the foundations for our journey together. I introduced you to the concept of manifestation. When you merge your vision and intention with the creative force of infinite intelligence, you can manifest what you truly desire.

This week is all about alignment, remembering who you are at the soul level. On Day 4, I mentioned that this is a 50-50 partnership with a Higher Power, and how the "work" you have to do is to prepare you for your manifestations. This part can be challenging, but remember that it is the part of the manifestation process that you *can* control. During the next part of this journey, we will start to peel back the layers of the onion to reveal who you are. It might be a lot to unpack, but take your time to read the content for today and allow yourself to sit with it.

On August 22, 2018, I launched the *Chase Wild Hearts* podcast. After I quit my corporate job, I started traveling the world full time. At the time, I had dreams to be a travel photographer, writer, and blogger. During my travels, I met people who were living their dream lives and making a living. It was the proof that I needed to confirm my belief that you can do what you love and make money doing it. I just had never met people like that before. In my life in New York, everyone I knew was doing something stable and secure. Being around people who had untethered themselves and allowed themselves to pursue their dreams and throw caution to the wind was life-changing for me. I wanted to interview these people and ask them about how they did it. Had they always believed they could achieve their dreams? Did their parents support them? By talking to the people I met for my podcast, I really felt like I was chasing them all over the world in search of how I could do what they were doing too, and also share this knowledge with my community back home.

I took my spiritual journey to the next level between 2018 and 2019 when I realized I didn't want to chase anymore. The energy of eagerly pursuing knowledge and people who seemed to have figured things out felt desperate and lacked trust. It was as if I was always asking myself, "Really, though?" without allowing myself to believe that what I was seeing was true. At the beginning of 2019, I wanted change, so I forced things to happen, because I didn't know any better. I also wanted to be more in alignment with my soul's purpose, but I didn't even fully understand what that meant.

Then one day, during a profoundly deep meditation, I heard a voice say, "awaken and align!" After my meditation, I looked up what these words meant, and they felt right. In the fall of 2019, I renamed my podcast *Awaken and Align* and changed its focus to reflect my own new mindset. Awaken and align are two calls to action. If you are awakened, you are an active participant in the unveiling of the truth of who you really are. To align is to connect your mind, body, and soul.

If you want the truth, you don't chase. You align and attract the things, people, and situations that are meant for you. Being attractive means that you are living your authentic life. The first step is knowing who you are and then living in your truth. Like I said previously, the Universe doesn't give you what you want, the Universe gives you who you are. The question is: Are you living in your authenticity?

When we were born, we *adopted*—or as Don Miguel Ruiz states, "agreed upon belief systems, paradigms, and inherited intergenerational traumas through epigenetics." As soon as we entered this world, our beliefs were being shaped by the people around us. Scientists have proven that between the ages of birth and seven years, a child's mind is like a sponge. By the time children turn seven, their personalities are fully developed throughout adulthood.

In 2020, I met a sacred geometrist, teacher, and friend through a Kundalini yoga retreat online. I reached out to her because I was interested in learning from her and wanted to collaborate. Her name is Sheetal, and she has been on my podcast, we have co-led energy workshops together, and she has coached me. She taught me about *maya*, the illusion. Essentially, we are all living in a dream. When she described this concept to me, it sounded like *The Matrix*. Yes, the movie with Keanu Reeves. Becoming aware of maya is quite similar to when Morpheus offers Neo the red pill or the blue pill. Spoiler alert: the red pill plugs him out of the matrix, the maya, the illusion. During 2020, I meditated on why there is so much separation, hate, and suffering in the world. What occurred to me during this time was that we have the power to co-create our collective dream—but also our hell.

We are tribal and communal beings. We need the pack to survive. Western culture is radical in its individualism, but we are not meant to live this way. Because of this, we are disconnected from one another, our Earth, and ultimately ourselves. When we decide to go outside of the confines of the pack, nuclear family, and what is expected of us culturally, we risk being rejected because we are seen as the "other."

We deeply crave acceptance—we want to be seen, heard, and validated. So, often we wear masks and hide who we are so that we are accepted by our people. Humans are wired for love and connection. Our souls deeply want to be loved and accepted, and sometimes, we abandon parts of ourselves in the pursuit of acceptance. But remember, manifesting is about being the creator of your own life: your dream life is of your own design. Manifesting means radiating your authenticity and creating a life on your own terms. And this is for the good of all involved. We are manifesting all the time, but are we manifesting based on other people's definitions of success? I want to challenge you and invite you to ask yourself, why do you want to manifest the things that you want? Do you think manifesting a partner will make you feel love? Do you believe manifesting money will make you feel rich? People think that they are manifesting *things*, but what people really want are states of being and emotional fulfillment.

For so much of our lives, we are told what to think and how to behave by our parents, teachers, mentors, media, and marketing. We are not guided to find ourselves. We are not taught to unlock our authentic selves. In childhood, we were not given the tools to understand who we are at the soul level. Our identities were formed for us by plugging into the matrix— the illusory world where everyone thinks the same way. It's not until we plug ourselves out because we want something more for our lives that we remember who we were as children, before we acquired the beliefs that clouded our judgment and pulled us away from our true desires. So often, we learn through "alternative" modalities to listen to our inner voice. Manifestation is just one of them.

One of the many limiting beliefs I had to work through and heal from in writing this book was the belief that there are already so many manifestation books out there. This topic has been written about extensively, made into movies, taught in courses. What else could I add to the manifestation movement? I had to keep coming back to my intention, which was to share my perspective and personal experiences in order to lend a different perspective on manifestation.

Your life experiences and everything that you've been through makes you unique. When I read people's natal charts, I see each person's soul print. Like snowflakes, no two natal charts are exactly alike, even identical twins. Each of us came here with a unique mission, destiny, or purpose—whatever you'd like to call it. Our life experiences, our struggles, and the actions we take also make us each unique. We are each born into wildness, and though the pressures of the world can chisel it away, it is our birthright. If you believe you have a vision for your life, are you sure? Can you look beyond the illusion of the "norm"— the things you feel you *should* do—and be confident that the vision and dream you have is what you truly desire?

Be aware and proactive about the pressures you are facing from your friends, the people you work with, the people you date. If your parents want you to get married and have kids and you don't want to, there isn't something wrong with you. If you don't want to have a nine-to-five job, you aren't necessarily being irresponsible. You can't force things to happen because you're turning twenty-nine and you're going through your Saturn return. Life is meant to be lived fully. Despite what we've felt unconsciously through the collective programming, there's no timeline and checklist for life.

The journey toward self-acceptance is being okay with your authenticity no matter what anyone else thinks or says to you. And believe me, that's difficult! Ninety-nine percent of the time, I am fully invested in my decisions and the way I've decided to live my life. I achieved "success" as it's traditionally defined, and then I gave it up to follow my dreams. But then there are those holidays when I'm faced with having to see the people from my past and family members who have chosen a traditional life. They boast about my cousin who is a doctor, my other cousin who is a physician's assistant, and my other cousin who has a finance job. A child who is a doctor is essentially every Korean parent's greatest dream. The last time I was present for this kind of display, I realized that I was never going to get that kind of acceptance or recognition from my family, and it hurt. It's usually a feeling I'm used to and can power through, but there are always moments of vulnerability when my ego is craving recognition and praise.

Maybe you've felt this way. If you've chosen the road less traveled, this probably resonates with you on a deep cellular level. The reassuring thing is that even when you have those moments when you crave the acceptance of others, it's your decision to follow your soul's calling that pulls you forward and keeps your fire burning regardless of any approval from the people around you. If you are one of the wild ones who decided to follow your soul's calling in lieu of others' validation, I'm sending you all of my love, because the love that radiates out of your heart is the energy that keeps the eternal flame of universal consciousness flowing. It's important that you continue to stoke that flame.

I understand why people don't pursue their dreams or why they quit at the first sign of a bump—it's a lonely journey. It's one that requires inner fortitude and a commitment to keep going even when nobody else is cheering you on.

I was thinking about Taylor Swift the other day. She is an exceptionally talented songwriter and composer. She had supportive parents who moved to Nashville to support her dreams. I keep thinking about all those artists we'll never know because they didn't have a family, community, friends, or teachers who believed in them and had resources to support them—we'll never get to see their creations or hear their music or read their words. We are the ones who lose out when we contribute to a world that fails to support the dreams of all individuals. When each of us shows up shining brightly, bringing our gifts to the collective, this is a more harmonious planet. Happy people treat others better—happiness is generative. Happy people create more things that make people happy.

In 2020, in the middle of a pandemic and the violence against marginalized groups like Black lives, everything that we as a society looked toward for security was falling apart. During 2020 and 2021, the south node was in Sagittarius, and Sagittarius is about our belief systems. The south node in astrology is a releasing point. So, in 2020, I decided to turn a new page and question *everything*. Why do we believe the things we believe in? If you have never asked yourself this question, our time together is the perfect time to do it, because you will realize a lot of the things we were taught are not true. This is what critical thinking and discernment are all about and what we need more of these days. Another aspect of Sagittarius is asking yourself philosophical questions and getting to the truth. The fears that prevent you from uncovering it are really only in your mind.

When we do not honor our true self—our soul's calling, what we love to do—we abandon a part of ourselves. But it isn't lost forever. You will forget about it for some time until one day when you'll be forced to find yourself again. When the world around you crumbles and you are suffering, you'll find that all the masks you wore, the things you thought were real, will be taken away and you will be forced to look at yourself. At first, you will feel lost because you will not recognize who you are. But when things are the most difficult, you'll be blessed by the capacity to see yourself clearly. All the things that you thought made you who you are—your title, the amount of money you made, the things you owned—will be revealed to be false and unsustainable because you when you remember who you are, there's no turning back.

But the good news is that you are a soul, you have the capacity to love deeply, and, just by existing, you can create worlds. You are part of an infinite intelligence that tells caterpillars when to cocoon, flowers to bloom, and the sun to rise. I hope that you'll take this time to absorb that information before a time of trial makes the choice for you. Take this day to meditate on your limitless possibility and strengthen yourself so that you can fall back on what's true and lasting: yourself.

Dream Discernment Meditation

Close your eyes and get into a meditative state, a space where you feel relaxed. Ask yourself the following questions: "What are my dreams? How do I see myself living my life?" Be totally honest with yourself. What comes up when you remove money, notoriety, and status from this situation? Whatever comes up, don't judge it. Explore it. It's also totally okay if money, notoriety, and status are in your dream, but this is a practice in connecting to what feels authentic to you. Write down the results of this meditation in your journal.

> ## GO DEEPER
>
> Get your natal chart read by an astrologer or an expert on human design, gene keys, numerology, or any system that can help you gain insight on yourself.

DAY 9
Giving and Receiving

"The mutual practice of giving and receiving is an everyday ritual when we know true love."
—bell hooks, *All About Love: New Visions*

NEWTON'S THIRD LAW OF MOTION states that for every action, there is an equal and opposite reaction, which is the same as the Hermetic Universal Law of Cause and Effect. We will explore the Hermetic laws of the universe in more depth in the coming weeks, but I wanted to bring your attention to *giving and receiving* as a basic law of the universe. Today is the day to investigate this law and begin believing in it beyond what you've already committed to.

This all might sound oversimplified, but the fact is you can manifest anything you want by simply giving of yourself wholeheartedly. As the spiritual text *A Course in Miracles* states, "To give and to receive are one in truth. I will receive what I am giving now."

When your mind (your thoughts and beliefs), heart (what you love), and soul (purpose) are in alignment, everything you do comes from a heart-centered place. You should fill your own cup first, because it will leave you feeling fulfilled. When you're in this state, you will have an abundance of energy and love to give freely and, in turn, you will receive what you truly desire.

It's mind-boggling how simple this can be. On Day 8, we abandoned our inauthenticity and desire to fit in with what we perceived as the norm. Today, it's time to consider that your life is a moving prayer and a devotion to your existence here on Earth. You are 400 billion in 1: that's how rare and unique you are. You're an exquisite being, and there is no one like you. You are a gift that you will give the Universe, and giving starts with radical authenticity: being completely honest with yourself about who you are and living in alignment with that truth, which are critical first steps toward manifesting.

Instead of focusing your attention on your manifestation goals, try the best you can to be more process oriented versus goal oriented. I want to help you to refocus your attention from an external goal back to yourself. I will use money as an example, because money is what many people want to manifest. Let's say your goal is manifesting $10K per month. First of all, money is just energy—it's a form of exchange for value. You give value and, in return, you receive money. So the question is: Do you value yourself? When you set a goal of $10K in a month, it's like the saying that your net worth is equal to your self-worth. Putting aside pay inequities and other systemic issues, are you asking for what you're worth? Are you charging a rate that reflects how much you've invested in yourself? There is a universal law that says that everything in nature eventually returns to homeostasis, or balance. There should be a balance between what you give and what you receive. If you're not making the dollar amount that you believe you should be making, there is a deeper underlying reason why you're not in the flow of money. That may be due to your beliefs, but I will ask you to put a pin in that line of thought because we will be investigating underlying beliefs and how they affect our manifestations next week.

I get it, we've all been there. I've been there. When I needed to manifest money immediately to pay my bills, I felt that I didn't have time to look deeper. Here is a cautionary tale for you: I would get my energy to the right vibration to manifest the money and then just as quickly as it came in, it would go. It was like a revolving door. I didn't even have a chance to enjoy the money in my bank account. I would be able to manifest money just to cover my bills, but I never felt wealthy. Later on, I learned about investing and how to grow my money, which I recommend you do as well. Learning about and being comfortable with wealth will help you get your energy to a place where you will feel that you are always in the flow. That was how, during my early attempts to manifest money, I realized that I wasn't really understanding manifestation at an energetic and spiritual level. You have full permission, not that you need it from me, to manifest in order to cover your basic needs, but eventually you will need to take the time to do the deeper work so that you can be in the flow and build a wealthy life.

Life is a journey, not a destination, so manifesting self-determined goals can be frustrating and unfulfilling. Once you manifest them, you'll want something else, and you will never feel full and whole. Instead, live in alignment and you will receive everything you want organically. Living for the destination is tantamount to death, so ask yourself, "What do I want the quality of my life to be between birth and death?" You want each moment of your life to be delicious, beautiful, and worth living—which is why it's so important to live in service of what your heart truly desires.

If you are not content or fulfilled, you will have nothing to give, and therefore, you will not receive—it's as simple as that. The more you give value to other people, the more people will support you. Your confidence will increase, you will give more, people will give more to you. Think about what you are passionate about and meditate on how you can share that with the people you love. That might be something straightforward (you love to paint and you create to share with the artistic community you respect) or it could be your passionate desire to help others through mutual aid. When you marry your passions with your life, you serve the world—and you'll automatically get paid for it, either in the literal sense or through the satisfaction you'll feel when you are living as your truest self.

If you have overcome something difficult, sharing that experience could also help people and serve a similar purpose. As Rumi wrote, "The wound is where the light enters." And in the words attributed to Joseph Campbell, "The cave you fear to enter holds the treasure you seek." It is usually the places where we have been wounded that hold the greatest treasures. When we have the courage to enter the cave and stand in the place where we received our wounds, we liberate ourselves from the power they have over us. When we share our stories, we also help free others who might find themselves in the same cave and under the spell and illusion of separateness. Sharing our stories is a service to others who might find solace in them. Start sharing and see how the Universe opens up to you.

Because money and wealth are energetic exchanges for what you give to the world, as long as you are living in alignment with your authentic truth—and only you can know what that is—then you will be rewarded in the form of money, wealth, and abundance. Wealth and notoriety follow people who are on their soul's path, so don't be surprised when you're met with abundance after you make life changes that reject the kind of inauthenticity we explored yesterday. The wealth you get could be a feeling of satisfaction when you wake up each day, a general belief that anything is possible, a sudden revenue stream, a bank account that never dips below a manageable level. Truth, happiness, and wealth are one and the same, and today is the day to internalize that belief.

You will know you are in alignment when you feel full and whole. You are happy and feel grateful. It doesn't mean you don't have bad days, but feeling whole and happy will help you move through the challenging times, it will bring you good things, and it will put you in the right space to continue on this manifestation journey.

Your Passions

Today is an opportunity to journal about what excites you most in this life. What are you passionate about? What is a problem that you've solved that could be of service to other people? What have you overcome in your life?

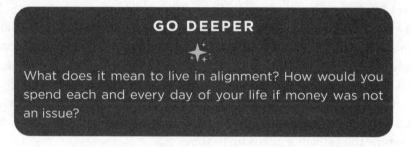

GO DEEPER

What does it mean to live in alignment? How would you spend each and every day of your life if money was not an issue?

DAY 10
Self-Worth and Love

"To be who you are and become what you are capable
of is the only goal worth living."
—Alvin Ailey

YESTERDAY, WE TALKED ABOUT giving and receiving. Today, we are adding a layer to that lesson. It's difficult to give if you don't feel worthy or if you don't feel like you have enough. Today is about filling up your own cup. We're going to explore ways to feel worthy and full without external validation.

Again, I want to remind you that while I've assigned these lessons to particular days, the manifestation process is not necessarily a linear journey. Cultivating your self-worth is a lifelong process, and while you may move on to the next lesson tomorrow, feel free to revisit today's theme and lessons whenever you feel called to.

Today, take a moment to think about how we manifest what we believe we deserve. Beyond just manifestation, the more you turn your gaze inward and focus on your self-worth, the more likely you are to ask for what you deserve and set firm boundaries. Your self-worth—how much you value yourself—is at the center of everything.

What we want is usually a direct reflection of what we value. Whenever I am looking at a client's astrological natal chart, I can tell right away how they like to spend their money and energy. A Sagittarius is probably spending a ton on travel and exploration, following their passions. A Cancer will want to make their home a cozy nest. And, more than just the sun signs, you can really see a person's values around money and worth reflected in the second house. My second house is ruled by Capricorn, so I know that I'm conservative in how I spend my money but I'm willing to make the investment if I know it will be worth it for the long term.

Even if you're skeptical about astrology, it's true that spending styles and the way we value our lives are wildly different—when it comes to the "right" way to direct your money and energy, it comes down to who you are. What we usually want to manifest is more of the things on which we spend our time, money, and energy. Take a look at your calendar and your bank account. This will give you a clear picture of what you value. Take in this information without judgment—just awareness. We need to have awareness in order to know what to change. This is an opportunity to evaluate whether the way in which you spend your money, time, and energy is in alignment with what you're manifesting.

I always tell my students that the best way to manifest anything and everything is to fully love yourself. When you want someone or something, that energy is often projected outward, and you create an energy of longing or desperation. Instead, shift your focus toward yourself. Start to take care of yourself, nurture yourself. You can do this through the simple task of getting more sleep, or eating nutritious foods, or pampering yourself with self-care activities.

Self-care does not just mean taking bubble baths, although that could be one act of self-care if a bubble bath is what will make you feel nurtured. Self-care is giving yourself the permission to be and do what you dream of, stand up for yourself, and ask for your worth. This is not selfish. This is necessary in order for you to feel whole. You cannot give to others if you do not give to yourself first. You have to feel so full and whole that you have more than enough to give to others. You have an abundance of love, energy, and time, and the people around you get the benefits.

I interviewed my Korean-American friend Chris Oh on my podcast, and she shared her inspiring manifestation story with me. Chris was a PR executive who worked with celebrities for fifteen years. With her permission, I'm sharing her story with you. After fifteen years of chasing job titles and promotional raises in the corporate world, she realized that she wasn't chasing what really mattered to her. She felt like she was losing control over her own destiny. She quit her job in the summer of 2019 to pursue a new chapter of her life that was more aligned with her authentic self. From that moment on, she vowed to chase every one of her dreams. She wanted to live a life that was not bound by anything other than her own compass. This journey led her to fulfill a twenty-year dream to live in London. To her disappointment, after a series of earnest trials to get a visa or sponsorship, Chris couldn't obtain any legal right to stay in that city, so her dream abruptly came to a halt and she had to go back to the States. Since she had left her NYC life and sold all of her belongings, she found herself at her parents' house during the pandemic. She knew deep down in her heart that this was not why she left her career and her established lifestyle in NYC. Chris knew intuitively that she belonged in Europe.

At the time, she didn't know that Portugal was the better decision—it truly was just a Plan B for her to get herself back to Europe. But the most beautiful thing about how everything transpired is that, looking back, she can connect the dots and know why London didn't work out. The Universe didn't want her in London because she was supposed to organically find her way to Portugal. To all of our collective envy, Chris is loving the lifestyle of slow living that characterizes Portugal as a country while connecting with the fascinating minds of the people who live there. She had intended to live in London, but because she was open to what the Universe had in store, her Plan B became her destiny. As she told me, "I can say this confidently because I took a risk, dove head-on into the unknown with the only thing I knew: that I had to trust my intuition."

My family and some of my friends who I grew up with don't think what I do is real work. They think of spirituality as a party trick or a phase, and to be honest, it might be a phase. I've given myself the permission over and over again to just do things that I love. And it doesn't matter to me if it keeps changing, because I'm having fun and I love what I do, and that's all that matters.

I believe that as spiritual beings, we came to Earth to experience life. To grow and expand. It is not in alignment with our souls to just do the same thing over and over again, living life in a loop. Suffering happens when we catch ourselves in a pattern but we don't know how to change or free ourselves. When we know our worth, we don't allow ourselves to merely be victims of our circumstances. We take the leap, knowing that the net will appear.

This is also why everyone will manifest something different for themselves. Each of us is driven by different things. Each of us has unique needs. Only you can know what the experience of being you feels like.

Manifesting requires radical acceptance of who you are and what you desire. The Latin origin of the word *radical* translates to "root." So it makes sense that radical acceptance comes from something deep within you, and it requires that you know yourself. As attributed to Aristotle, "knowing yourself is the beginning of all wisdom." When you live your life with authenticity, whatever is meant for you will never be withheld from you.

Mirror Work

This exercise was developed by legendary spirituality writer Louise Hay. Stand in front of a mirror. Take a deep breath and repeat an affirmation to yourself ten times while you look into your eyes. Try: "I am worthy of everything I desire." You can also repeat any other affirmations that you feel called to.

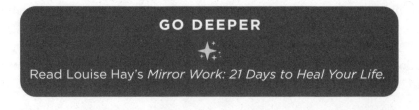

GO DEEPER

Read Louise Hay's *Mirror Work: 21 Days to Heal Your Life.*

DAY 11
Living in the Present Moment

"Realize deeply that the present moment is all you ever have."
—Eckhart Tolle, *The Power of Now*

FROM DAYS 4 AND 5 on Week 1 of this journey, you have been doing some kind of daily ritual and devotion to a Higher Power. A daily devotion in the form of prayer and meditation helps your mind, body, and soul come into alignment in the present moment. Today is all about living in that present moment, and what that practice can do for you. Your life is a tapestry of interwoven moments that create the story of your own design. Your life can only be savored in the moment to moment. Here, in the present moment, is when you can experience serendipity and events that are beyond your wildest imagination, because you couldn't have planned them. The present moment is where all the magic lies.

During the fall of 2021, I had a huge epiphany. I realized I had manifested something that I had been thinking about but didn't realize was possible: *this book*! To get into the right headspace for manifesting, I had to get into my creative energy. I would take long stretches of time off from social media, and I was very mindful of what I was watching. I filled my mind with art, poetry, and nature. I would take myself out on dates, which is a practice I learned from Julia Cameron's *The Artist's Way*. I would reread my favorite books that got me believing in manifestation in the first place.

Think of yourself as an energy bank. Notice your inputs and outputs and how they affect your mood, vitality, and energy levels. Does the way you're living inspire you or make you feel shitty? You've worked toward creating your reality by being in the present moment, which required you to cultivate radical acceptance of the present moment and take responsibility for your life. The next step is healing.

We cannot move forward without being conscious of the present, and we can't be in the present if we keep looking back at the past. Tomorrow becomes now, and if we live in the past, it becomes our now instead. Time is not linear—it's all happening simultaneously. Our ego just perceives time as linear, and that's not a bad thing. We are humans living in this physical reality, and we need an organized way of thinking about our lives. But manifestation doesn't have to be years in the making. Everything is energy. It can happen now.

When I worked at my corporate job—and I'm sure many of you can relate—I used to *live* for the weekends. All of my joy, excitement, and lust for life was reserved for the weekends. That meant that five days out of every seven were never spent in the present moment. I also lived for the big milestones in my life, rushing past the present moment to get to that vacation or birthday or promotion. I was always planning, moving, and traveling to go somewhere else, and never fully content with where I was just in the moment. Like so many wanderers out there, 2020 made me be still for the first time in my life and face all my feelings and thoughts. I didn't understand that a life worth living is made up of small moments in between the milestones.

Whenever I get into a state of looking back or forward and not being in the present moment, I ask myself something that my friend Venika asked me: "What needs to happen or appear in your life right now to make you feel what you want to feel?" What she was asking me was: What do I feel like I'm missing? It made me name the emotion I was feeling, which I now realize was *scarcity*. When I'm in the present moment, I can fully appreciate everything that I currently have. What you focus on expands, and part of manifesting is being grateful for what you already have. If you're living in the past or projecting yourself into the future, you'll be living in scarcity.

In Dr. Joe Dispenza's *Becoming Supernatural,* he devotes an entire chapter to the importance of being in the present moment. He explains why this state is crucial to creating a different reality, because it allows you to tap into the quantum field that can only be accessed when you train your body to be in the infinite present moment. As he writes, "Every time you keep settling your body back to the present moment, like training a dog to sit, you are reconditioning your body to a new mind." The practice of being present is something that can—and should—be cultivated. It doesn't necessarily come naturally!

I really got this message when I watched the Pixar movie *Soul*. Throughout the story, Joe Gardner goes through many obstacles to make his dream a reality. Joe tries to accomplish this in his human life and again when he has the chance in a reincarnated body. He has tunnel vision and believes playing at one particular jazz club is his ultimate goal, but when he finally accomplishes this, the happiness and fulfillment that he feels falls short of his expectations. He reflects back on his life and he realizes that the whole point of his existence was about experiencing each moment and building a friendship with 22, a soul in training. It is only when he feels fully in the present that he comes to this realization. You may be surprised by the realizations you'll have when you stop reaching for a goal in the future or searching through the remnants of the past for answers.

Free Your Mind

Learning to be in the present can be a lengthy process. So, set yourself up for success as you begin by doing an inventory of your inputs and outputs in any given day. What are you reading or watching? Who are you interacting with?

A good first step is taking a digital detox for one day. For example, turn off your phone and put it away; don't watch the news, if you have the luxury; take the day off your laptop. The goal is to have little to no blue light exposure for one whole day. Notice how much mental space there is for you to think and create. Every time you reach for your phone or the TV remote, take a deep breath and feel yourself in the present moment. You'll find that the craving to scroll fades over the course of a day—you may find it hard to believe, but give it a try.

GO DEEPER

Take a digital detox for one week, or through the rest of this journey.

DAY 12
Rewilding

"And into the woods I go, to lose my mind and find my soul."
—Attributed to John Muir

HAVE YOU EVER NOTICED that nature is green? When we think of nature, we think of green trees and abundant growth, green grass, green leaves. In the same way, so many symbols of creativity and abundance are related to the color green: the heart chakra is green, US paper money is green. In early modern Europe, the color green was associated with wealth, banks, and the gentry. Green jade is tied to wealth and abundance, along with divine wisdom and harmony. It's not a coincidence.

Modern civilizations are out of sync with nature and the natural cycles of the life, death, and rebirth process of transformation. With the advancement of technology comes great progress, but our reliance on technology is also detrimental to our natural way of being. We have become disconnected from ourselves, our bodies, and our internal clocks. For example, during the winter months, we should be more *yin*—or receptive. It's a time to rest and conserve our energy. But since we have electricity, light, and technology, nothing can stop us from burning the proverbial midnight oil.

If we never left our climate-controlled homes, we'd barely know it was winter at all. With advancements in farming and agriculture, we can eat strawberries all year round, and because we are so far removed from the supply chain, we often don't understand what it takes to grow the food we eat and how many hands need to handle our products before they get to us. This kind of massive disconnect on all levels has a real effect on our energetic selves, and it can make the process of manifestation that much more difficult.

Part of tuning in to creative energy is learning how to rewild ourselves. This means syncing ourselves back into natural cycles. It means retraining our bodies so that they know when to take action and when to rest. It means reestablishing that there is a time to create, die, rebirth, and transform.

In many ancient cultures, the symbolism of the Ouroboros is aligned with infinity, wholeness, and the cyclical nature of our lives. The Ouroboros is an image of a serpent in a circular formation eating its own tail. The Ouroboros is a visual metaphor for life. Life is predicated on a death and rebirth process—an alchemical process of being rebirthed from what is dead. I have traveled to more than fifty-eight countries around the world, and each funeral or burial service I've witnessed was such an eye-opening experience. Different cultures process death in so many different ways, and the variety of rituals associated with the end of life are staggering. When I visited Indonesia, I learned that they see death as a rite of passage from a human embodiment back to the Source. When someone dies, the community comes together to mourn and to celebrate the person's human life.

Being in nature always connects me to the energy of oneness that ties us all. Like Eywa from the movie *Avatar* remarks, when asked about the name of the guiding force of Pandora, "Who's Eywa? Only their deity! Their goddess, made up of all living things." It's the circle of life from *The Lion King* and the spirits introduced by Grandmother Willow in *Pocahontas*. This universal natural energy is a concept repeated over and over again in the stories we tell each other.

This is an especially valuable concept for women and for anyone who wishes to identify with the feminine principle in themselves. As Clarissa

Pinkola Estés writes in her book *Women Who Run with the Wolves*, "When women reassert their relationship with the wildish nature, they are gifted with a permanent and internal watcher, a knower, a visionary, an oracle, an inspiratrice, an intuitive, a maker, a creator, an inventor, and a listener, who guide, suggest, and urge vibrant life in the inner and outer worlds." She further describes how that figure—the wild teacher, wild mother, wild mentor—stays with them to support their inner and outer lives. The natural world is relentless and unchanging, and if you align yourself with its power, you gain an unending support.

The best way to heal your burnout and remind yourself to slow down is to be in nature. When you slow down, you can hear the inner calling of your soul. You can quiet your erratic mind and ground your energies to the earth. The earth reminds us of how abundance is all around us and inherently within us, as we are part of this earth. Our bodies will die and decompose into the earth one day: our cells become a part of the soil, which becomes fertile for new life. Just as we are stardust, we are a part of the life and death process of this earthly plane as well.

We live in a society and culture that often values the logical, intellectual mind versus the intuitive one. Intuition—which cannot be quantified or given evidential proof—is our wild, innate state of being. We rely on our intuition to create. I'm American, which is a capitalistic society that often preaches that more is better and faster is better. I've learned that this is a fallacy. Faster and quicker helps you to be distracted from what really matters in life, and unlike the natural world, it is unsustainable.

New York City is the capital of efficiency, and when I lived there, I felt like I had to move fast enough to keep up with its tempo. Walking fast, talking fast, fast food, fast everything—during the ten years I lived in the city, everything was a blur because I was always on the move. To where? I'm still not sure. I don't want to rush through my life anymore. I want to move through life slowly and intentionally. And I want the same for you.

Take this day not just to reconnect with nature, but to consider the desires that animate you in everyday life. Are you being driven forward by the beat of *more, more, more,* or are the things that motivate you organic and aligned with your true purpose? In her book *The Soul of Money*, author Lynne Twist writes, "The greatest teacher of sufficiency is nature and the natural laws of the earth." She also asks whether we can change our relationship with money and reconsider the belief that more is better. She asks us to consider reinvestigating our understanding of what is already in our lives, writing, "Rather than growth being external in acquiring and accumulating money or things, can we redefine growth to see it as a recognition of and appreciation for what we already have?" What does growth mean to you? Who will you be once you have grown, and what will you need to do to get there?

Forest Bathing

Shinrin-yoku, translated into English, means "forest bathing." Taking a leisurely walk in a forest is a therapeutic reprieve from modern life. It was developed in Japan in the 1980s as preventive health care and is considered to be healing in Japanese medicine. Take a thirty-minute walk in nature, preferably in a forest if one is available to you. Take note of what you see and how the experience makes you feel. Try not to judge or evaluate—let nature speak to you. Whatever you experience will be worthwhile and meaningful.

GO DEEPER

Read *Women Who Run With the Wolves* by Clarissa Pinkola Estés. Go on a hike or visit a nature preserve for the day. If you have been thinking of visiting a natural wonder that is nearby but have just never "had the time," take the time today.

DAY 13
Joy and Play

"There is no way to repress pleasure and
expect liberation, satisfaction, or joy."
—Adrienne Maree Brown,
Pleasure Activism: The Politics of Feeling Good

I BELIEVE WE ARE closest to our manifestation and creative energy when we are having fun and when we are joyful. I'm sure you've felt pure bliss and pleasure at one point in your life. When was that? Think about when you last forgot what time it was because you were so in the moment. When was the last time you were having so much fun that you didn't even look at your phone?

If you ask anyone "What do you want in life?" most people will say happiness or some form of joy. It's in our American Constitution: *life, liberty, and the pursuit of happiness*. So why does it sometimes seem like everyone is miserable? I believe it's our limiting beliefs on what it takes to live our dream lives. Perhaps you are thinking—consciously or subconsciously—that successful manifestation might require some kind of major effort. But I am here to tell you that when you manifest successfully, the process is full of ease and joy. We just have to dispense with the belief that we are more worthy of something if we worked hard for it. Hard work has nothing to do with it!

When we manifest, we desire something, and we want it to come into our lives. We often focus on a negative thing not being there—the absence of it. We focus on the *lack*, which perpetuates our feelings of scarcity. The secret is that we were taught the opposite of what we should actually be doing. Let me explain. So often, we are taught to look outside of ourselves for what we want—that's everything, including but not limited to joy, love, validation, and on and on. We default to believing that everything we want is *out there* when, in reality, everything we want is inside of us. In other words: *as within, so without*. Luckily, the antidote to this limiting belief is—fun! It is joy, pleasure, and play. Take this day to love your life, because that energy is magnetic.

Like attracts like—that's the main tenet of the Law of Attraction. Think about that for a second: Would you be attracted to fun or to scarcity? When I feel creatively stagnant, bored, or apathetic, I know that I have to change up the energy. When you're in that mindset or emotional state, you will miss the miracles around you. You might also miss the signs and synchronicities the Universe is sending you. So, if you're feeling limited, instead of defaulting to lack, change it up and just have fun. I know this might seem tactless during times when there seems to be so much suffering in the world, but I want to remind you that injecting more joy in your life is the antidote to suffering, and it does not disrespect what other people are going through.

This step requires you to know what brings you joy. You would be surprised at the number of people who come to me and don't know. Joy is something that is often put on hold when we become adults, because we are busy achieving and working. When I studied abroad in Spain, my host family would always point out to me that Americans live to work versus work to live. I always thought it was ironic and cruel that most baby boomers like my parents worked their whole lives, waiting until retirement to enjoy themselves. My parents are retired now and they are not as nimble as they used to be, so there are many things that would have brought them joy when they were younger that they aren't able to do now. I think about all the elders who waited until they were retired to live their lives but then died before they were able to reap the rewards of their hard-earned savings. I believe that cultivating a life in which we can experience joy *right now* is integral for being able to successfully manifest the reality you are working toward.

And it's not just joy that will ultimately help us: if we allow ourselves to fully feel the spectrum of our emotions, we can use it as a guidance system to give us information. There's a lot to learn from how you feel if you are willing to investigate more deeply. You have felt feelings of contraction like anger, resentment, and doubt. And likewise, when you are joyful you will feel expansive emotions like ecstasy, enlightenment, and compassion. We are constantly going through the ebb and flow of emotions. This is not about bypassing your feelings and perpetuating toxic positivity—living only in joy at the expense of everything else—but if you can be honest about your feelings, it's easier to understand what they're truly trying to tell you. When you do more things that bring you joy, you feel liberated. That is the energy you want to cultivate in your life. We sometimes avoid doing the things we want to do because we believe we must please the people around us. We don't enforce our boundaries, or we don't communicate. But if you take the opportunity to live based on how you feel, you will know what you want. Today, ask yourself, "Does what I am doing bring me joy? Or do I feel contracted?"

Playful Questioning

Ask yourself the following questions:

- ★ What brings me joy?
- ★ What did I love to do as a child?
- ★ What gets me excited?
- ★ What would I do for free?

Write down the answers in a journal or meditate on them as you commit to a playful practice, like star gazing, bouncing on a trampoline, jumping rope, or climbing a tree. Play a board game you haven't pulled out of the closet since you were six, try a coloring book, squish some clay, or think about some other activity that engaged you when you were small. Today's the day to revisit it.

GO DEEPER

Read *Pleasure Activism* by Adrienne Maree Brown. Take yourself out on a playdate or try it out with your loved one or friend.

DAY 14
Act As If

"All you can possibly need or desire is already yours. Call your desires into being by imagining and feeling your wish fulfilled."
—Neville Goddard

THE VERY FIRST manifestation book I read was *Ask and It Is Given* by Esther and Jerry Hicks. I watched *The Secret* like so many others, but *Ask and It Is Given* was my first real introduction into this practice. I bought the book in 2017. I have even been to an Esther Hicks event with my mom. It was so interesting to see Esther channel Abraham Hicks in person, and I do believe in channelers after having seen it. What piqued my interest about the book was that it all seemed so easy. You get your vibration right by matching the vibration of the thing that you want. In case you've never read the book, I want to catch you up to speed. In Chapter 10, you learned the three steps to whatever you want to be, do, or have.

Step 1 (your work): You ask. Duh!
Step 2 (not your work): The answer is given.
Step 3 (your work): You receive and allow the answer
  (you let it in).

This looks easy on paper, but I found it to be challenging to constantly keep my vibration in check. The consensus between me and my friends who were also into manifestation was the same: there are so many other variables to consider that can't be bypassed.

Obviously, I believe in this process, but for a long time, I felt like something was missing when I tried it. I now know that that something was healing my beliefs and perceptions. You see, if you can't even believe it's possible, then when you ask, you will automatically be filled with doubt. I'm not saying you must be completely doubt-free, but you have to get to a place where you don't allow self-sabotage from your doubts to prevent you from being able to successfully manifest.

Another thing to note is that there isn't any mention of intergenerational trauma and oppression in messages from Abraham. When your epigenetic lineage has only known survival, it's not hard to see that thoughts might not always become things. I believe that a more holistic and inclusive process for manifestation has to account for these issues.

During these last fourteen days, we talked about your dreams, intentions, visions, and alignment. This was all to prep you for the juiciest part of the work. In the next week, you will revisit your past, reflect on your mindset and beliefs, and uncover your mind, body, soul, energy, and emotions. At first, it might seem like each of these is isolated. You might even contemplate the week ahead and feel overwhelmed at everything that you have to consider. There will be time for integration—actually, you must take time to integrate. But first, what I want you to realize is that everything is connected. Your feelings are affected by your thoughts; your fears are activated by your environment and your past. Your actions are dictated by either fear or love.

So many of us have made decisions in our lives based on fear and the illusion of scarcity. It's so easy to choose safety and security over our dreams. There's no shame in this game, because I've done it myself—I'd go so far as to say we've all done it. Often, when we make fear-based decisions, it's because we didn't know there was another way. But once you awaken to something, there's no going back.

As I mentioned in the beginning, the Universe gives you who you are, not what you want. The energy of what you seek must radiate from within you. You must integrate your thoughts, beliefs, feelings, actions, and energy and then point them toward the things you want. And to do that effectively, you must practice discernment and know when to be in the yin and when to be in the yang—when to give and when to receive.

To put it simply, the biggest part of manifestation is faith. We will talk more about that during the coming weeks. Faith requires you to believe more in what you don't see than what you do see. You have to believe without a shadow of a doubt that your life is changing, even though your environment and your surroundings might not yet show you the evidence of your manifestation.

The mind, which is aligned with the element of Air, is quick. You can think thoughts in a millisecond. Vision and passion come next—that's the Fire element. Emotions are the most important part of this process, because without feeling, there's no energy behind what you desire. That is why feeling what it's like, or acting *as if*, is the most important part of manifestation: the Water element. Physical matter and the body—Earth elements—move at a slower pace. Sometimes manifestations take longer than the mind wants them to come, which is why it's so important to be able to live in the feeling of the present moment, before the physical world catches up with it. We can experience the manifestation immediately by feeling it.

Most humans don't understand that nothing in nature is linear, not even time. We process our lives through the past, present, and future. But if you can tap into the infinite potential of the Higher Power, you will understand that there is a divine timing to everything that might not correspond to *happened*, *is happening*, or *will happen*.

Our human eyes can only see 0.0035 percent of the entire electromagnetic spectrum. There is so much we can't see, but it all exists in the unified field. Your energy just isn't matched to the vibration of it—yet. You don't see the full spectrum of what is available to you yet, not because you're not good enough or that you've done something wrong, but because your range is limited. I always try to remind myself that when I don't get something, it's either because it's not the right time, it's not for me, or something better is on the way.

This morning, my friend asked me what I was currently manifesting, and I will let you all know what it is if it comes into my physical reality by the time this book is published. I told her what it was—which I don't usually do, because I like to keep my manifestations sacred within me until they are birthed—but something came over me and I felt the need to share it with her. It was partially because my manifestation needs the help of others.

After I told her, my friend said, "I never knew you wanted to do that." My reply was that, until recently, I had never allowed myself to believe that it was possible. This manifestation was always a dream in the back of my mind, but I never knew it was in the realm of possibility. After I spoke to her and was able to say it out loud, it made my manifestation feel more real, and I knew it would happen, no matter what. I've already started the process of imagining myself doing it. What it would feel like. What the experience would be like. And in terms of action, I'm taking the necessary steps to network and connect with people who can help me. Most of all, I'm going to allow Spirit to help—by bringing to me the right people and circumstances. I don't have a deadline, and I'm open to how it all happens.

I'm writing this during a time in my life when I'm manifesting and calling in my soulmate. This is why being in alignment is so important, because my heart is saying yes but my mind is saying no. I'm sending out conflicting energies. This is also the reason why in the past I was attracting people who were not in alignment with me. My heart is longing for a deep connection with someone, but my tendency is to project all my fears into my thoughts and behaviors. The end product of this is that I'm not as open and not in the right space to give people a chance. When I doubt, other people sense the iciness of my heart. Doubt allows my mind to think back to my previous heartbreaks and fear that I'll feel that pain again, and so I project my fears into the future. This happens even when I don't consciously intend for it to. Instead of looking outward and blaming the "bad dates" I've had (which is always so tempting!), I am taking the time to heal from my past and allow my heart to connect to my mind and be in alignment.

I personally believe that we have more than one soulmate, which means that I don't believe there is just one person for us. If you do believe that there's one person out there for you, I respect your beliefs. But I believe that two of my exes were my soulmates. On Day 32, I will talk about your soul family and how integral they can be in supporting you and the creation of your dreams. I believe soulmates are a part of our soul family. They are our romantic and platonic partners who help us grow.

The only advice I can give about manifesting your soulmate is to feel whole and happy being alone. You read that right: be happy single. We will talk more about wholeness on Day 29, but I'm giving you a preview. Just before I started dating each of my soulmates, I remember being so happy. I was having so much fun and living my life. Unlike my friends who were on the hunt to get married, I didn't wait for a romantic partner before I traveled, ate at amazing restaurants, and explored new locales. I did it alone. I know, it's so cliché to say that when you're not looking for love, that's when it finds you. But I really believe that this phenomenon happens because energetically, love finds you when you're attractive, and when you love your life, you are attractive. I was living my best, most authentic and happy life, and love was attracted to that energy.

I can already hear some of you saying, "But I'm doing that, and I still have not manifested 'the one'!" My answer to that is: keep reading. In the coming days, we'll look at your underlying beliefs. So whether you're looking for "the one" or $10,000 in the bank, you'll have to take the time and do the work to be magnetic. But don't worry, you'll have the space to do that as we move forward in this journey together!

Meditation for Preparing to Manifest

Sit in a comfortable position. Feel your sit bones firmly grounded to the floor and the crown of your head rooting up to the heart of the sky. Make sure your spine is straight and you're breathing in a rhythmic motion. Inhale through the nose for a count of three, hold for four, and exhale for five counts out through the mouth. Do this for three minutes. Feel the present moment and the expansiveness of the present moment. Allow the thoughts to enter your mind. Be aware of them and allow them to pass like drifting clouds. Focus your attention on the breath. Notice where you feel contracted in your body. Breathe into that area of your body. Scan your body, and do this for any other areas until you feel light and free. Now, bring into your mind's eye what it looks like to have your manifestation at the forefront of your consciousness. Allow your mind to go there. Take mental notes of what this vision looks like. Now, notice the feeling and sensations in your body as you are visualizing this manifestation. Be here as if it's happening right now. Take as long as you need to be in the feeling of it. Stay here for ten minutes. When you feel it, you can slowly bring more awareness into your physical body. Stretch your legs and shake out your wrists. Slowly open your eyes.

When you come out of your meditation, journal what you need to believe, feel, and do to bridge the gap to who you want to become. What do you need to let go of to become that version of you? You bridge the gap by being it now.

GO DEEPER

Make the feeling real and visceral by doing it. Go test drive your dream car, go to an open house, act *as if*.

Week 3

DAYS 15–21

Healing Our Beliefs

We have set our sights on our new reality and placed ourselves in alignment with our desires. This week is all about going inward and doing a complete inventory of our belief systems—conscious and unconscious—as well as our fears and anxieties, the trauma we have carried through our family lineage, and any other limitations that may be holding us back. On Day 21, we will perform a ritual of release that will free us and encourage us to move forward in joy and wholeness.

DAY 15
Honoring the Past

"History is not the past. It is the present. We carry our history with us. We are our history."
—James Baldwin, *I Am Not Your Negro*

THIS WEEK, WE ARE taking a journey down into your underworld—metaphorically of course. If you've never done this kind of work before, I am here supporting you. I am sending you loving energy now, and because energy moves through time and space, just know that I'm here with you. I want to let you know that healing may be challenging, but it's so worth it. During this process, if you feel triggered, that is completely normal and okay. Give yourself some grace and compassion.

I believe you are simultaneously healing your past while creating a better future. You might have heard in the spiritual community that we are multidimensional beings. I believe we are spiritual beings having a human experience and, because of this, we have the capacity to create a different future for ourselves by healing. In the first week of this journey, I had you think about your dream and your vision, because we need the strength of our vision to pull us forward. If we are just healing and looking to the past, we will lose steam. It's important to be healing, doing the work, and unlearning while simultaneously holding the vision for a better future. This is crucial! You don't have to heal first and then you receive your blessing. It doesn't work like that. This is a journey, not a destination.

Our consciousness is tuned into this current reality that we have all co-created together. This is what Carl Jung termed "the collective unconscious." There is another timeline out there where you are living the life of your dreams, or even several timelines! We can shift our focus to that timeline. I'm sure you've heard the saying that nothing ever changes because nothing ever changes. You are manifesting right now. I hope we are on the same page when I say that you want to manifest something different—better, even. So, something within you must change. Whether it's a shift in your perspective, your beliefs, your neural pathways, or all of the above. From Week 2, we talked about how your outer realm is a reflection of your inner realm. Something internally must shift and, therefore, we must find out what it is.

What you know is not true in the present moment—it was true only in the past.

What's true in this present moment is only what you decide to be true. You can heal your past by healing your perception of it.

The historical past is gone and it does not have to dictate your future. This is in no way excusing the things that happened to you, but to free yourself from the resentment, anger, and the heaviness that prevents us from transcending our own situation, we must let go of what has happened to us.

Healing is not linear. We go through ebbs and flows. It's okay to let go and say goodbye. Often, the biggest obstacle to healing is that we are not ready to let go of what we know so that we can create space for what's to come, because we are afraid of the emptiness. When you let go of what you knew, what will take its place? The ego wants control because it desires self-preservation, so it habitually recalls memories from the past to predict the future. Your future is projected solely from things that have already happened, how accurate is it, really? Another friendly reminder: if you want to create something different from your past, you must step into the unknown. Your ego will go wild at the thought of not knowing, but this is when you call upon your higher self for guidance. The unknown is empty and dark, but life is created in the darkness, and we have to be willing to be in the vastness of that space.

Newton's first law of thermodynamics states that energy cannot be either created or destroyed. That means that once you let go of something, something else will inevitably take its place. Stepping into the unknown is like Scorpio energy, which is the season in which I'm writing this section of this book. People tend to focus on the "death" part of Scorpio energy, since that sign tends to be associated with darkness and the end, but it's important to remember that within death is rebirth. Death is the catalyst for transformation. The Universe wants us to let go of our grip, and that catalyst loosens it. Sometimes, we romanticize the past or we fixate on that person who should not have done that thing to us. We feel anger and resentment. But keep going back to the universal laws. What we feel, we attract, so it's in your best interest to do your part and heal the past so that you can move forward. We are meant to flow with life and extract the wisdom from each experience, and to not hold on and define ourselves based on what happened in the past.

This is where the spiritual work comes in. If you began this process expecting rainbows and butterflies, that's not the whole story. The healing we do to put ourselves in the right place for manifestation is immensely fulfilling. But the act of bringing our dreams into reality also requires dark nights of the soul. The journey is all about unfolding the layers of who we are to find our unique essential truth. We are infinite beings in a temporary skin who have the capacity to create our lives. We just tend to forget that, either through social conditioning, heartbreak, or someone making us feel small. This journey is just as much about remembering who you are as it is about manifesting—you can't do one without the other.

In 2016, I had a run-in with an ex-boyfriend that was so upsetting I couldn't face my own feelings—I just shoved them all down so that I didn't even feel anything at all. I was so cut off from my emotions that I went through my days feeling completely numb. To try to recuperate, I went to Santa Fe, New Mexico, on a mother-daughter trip. One night during the trip, five glasses of wine in, I found myself taking a bath alone, listening to Adele's song "Hello," and crying my eyes out for an hour straight before I finally asked myself what needed to change about this situation. I wanted someone to love me desperately, but I also felt out of control. So at that moment, I knew that I had to address my grief before I did anything, and certainly before I could think about manifesting a new relationship.

You don't attract what you want, you attract who you are, so in essence, if you want to attract something different into your life, something has to change. The old you has to die. This is metaphorical, of course. "But the old Taylor can't come to the phone right now / Why? Oh, 'cause she's dead." That line from Taylor Swift's song "Look What You Made Me Do" is such a good example of this. Taylor let go of the old version of herself—the one who pleases people and does things to be validated by others. And the new version of herself has the power to do what she wants.

To go through the death-and-rebirth phase, you'll have to let go of the parts of yourself that no longer fit the version of you that you need to become in order to manifest. I also like to call this the "phoenixing" moment when you metaphorically burn away the parts of you that you no longer need and then you are reborn from your ashes. If we have the courage to walk away and create more space, we won't have to reckon with that undesirable excess material and will be completely able to receive what the Universe will give us. Don't let yourself end up staying at that desk job you hate for ten more years. Don't stay with your partner if your values no longer align. We stay in situations even though we know we should walk away, because the human urge is to stick with knowing because not knowing—and stepping out into the unknown—is so terrifying.

Letting go and releasing are quite painful—there is a grieving process that nobody talks about when you leave something behind. Part of you knows nothing will ever be the same again, even if logically you know that this thing no longer serves you. During the pandemic, many of us realized that we had to make changes in our lives—a global crisis can do that! Lockdowns and quarantines gave us permission to not engage in distractions. For my part, being in "hermit mode" allowed me to see who was worth my energy and who was not. I realized I needed more from my relationships; those that didn't fit into my new values had to be released. When death lingers at the forefront of our collective consciousness, there is no time for superficiality.

To call in relationships where you feel safe and secure, you'll have to set firm boundaries on the kinds of people you let into your orbit. The places that you envision yourself going, the kinds of things that you want to do, must no longer include people who make you feel small and question your goals.

Part of manifestation is trusting in the unknown—taking a leap into the Universe knowing that it will catch you without exactly understanding how. It's the fool card in tarot. It's when you have more belief in your vision than you do in your fears of the unknown. Today is your invitation to let in that feeling and make the leap out into the dark without understanding quite what will happen when you get there.

Preparing Yourself for Release

Write down a memory from the past that you can't let go of that you intend to let go of. Save it for a release ceremony in the coming days.

GO DEEPER

Growth comes from discomfort. I hope you know that if you're going through a difficult time right now, you are on the cusp of giving birth to a new beginning. Watch the YouTube video of Rabbi Dr. Abraham Twerski talking about lobsters and growing through adversity. Watch a video of butterflies emerging from the chrysalis. Take the time to be grateful and excited for the transition that you're about to go through, even if you feel scared or uncomfortable.

DAY 16
Forgiveness

"There is no peace without forgiveness. Attack thoughts towards
others are attack thoughts towards ourselves.
The first step in forgiveness is the willingness to forgive."
—Marianne Williamson, *Illuminata*

TODAY, WE WILL TALK about forgiveness, which can be elusive for so many of us. But forgiveness is the thing that will set us free. First of all, if you feel resistance toward the concept of forgiving, that's normal. I invite you to lean in to the resistance and investigate more deeply today. We are going to bypass the blockage by becoming expansive and identifying those that we must forgive in order to move forward.

To have the capacity to create, we must forgive all the people who said we couldn't do it or who limited us in some way—for example, parents, teachers, or guidance counselors. My parents didn't allow me to go to art school, and I felt like a part of me shut down. I had to forgive them to take the next steps in my own life. You may have had painful experiences in your past that could still be blocking you in so many different ways. The pathway to liberation is forgiveness, but that might be the last thing you want to do. It's not uncommon to get stuck thinking, *How could they get away with it?* You may feel like nobody was a witness to your pain—that if you forgive, they will continue with their lives without suffering any repercussions at all.

It may seem counterintuitive, but first, forgive yourself. Forgive yourself for allowing their opinions and beliefs to enter your conscious awareness. In his book *The Four Agreements*—which I recommend to everyone—Don Miguel Ruiz writes, "Whenever we hear an opinion and believe it, we make an agreement, and it becomes part of our belief system."

For my part, I had to forgive my parents for saying things like "Artists don't make any money" and "That's not being realistic" when I begged to go to art school. I forgave my guidance counselor and teachers, who agreed with my parents. And then I forgave myself for accepting those beliefs. I recognized that the eighteen-year-old me didn't know who she was but wanted to find out. She wanted to explore this world and all of the opportunities out there. But she also didn't want to disappoint her parents and the people around her. In this society, there's so much pressure to go to college as a necessary rite of passage, but by now opinions on it are more nuanced. So many more people know that a college degree does not equal success. But at the time, there was immense pressure on everyone involved, because they believed the choice to go to a "normal" college would put me on the right track. So I recognize that everyone was in a difficult situation and made the choices that they felt were available to them.

Like healing, forgiveness is not linear—and that's okay. Perhaps you thought you had forgiven and moved on from things that happened to you during childhood, but you were triggered unexpectedly and you felt anger or fear or sadness when you felt like you had released it long ago. When the triggers come back again, you might feel like you haven't fully healed yet or that you've failed at forgiving. While it's true that these feelings resurfacing gives you another opportunity to heal more deeply—it doesn't make it any easier, does it? I can't blame you for not wanting another opportunity at transmuting wounds that had lain dormant for many years. It's hard and painful. Still, the fact of the matter is that as you grow, these old wounds may continue to reopen. Traumatic memories from childhood may resurface to help you soothe your inner child as an adult. Try your best not to run from these feelings: sit with them.

There are practical reasons for working through these emotions. If you hold on to resentment and anger, you will relive the past over and over again, and it will be so hard to escape from the pain, especially if you are trying to grow as a human being. The stress response your body experiences when you struggle with resentment—the release of stress hormones such as adrenaline and cortisol—makes it very difficult, if not impossible, to manifest. Physiological effects aside, how can you experience what you desire in the future if your mind and your body are stuck in the past?

The ancient Hawaiian prayer Ho'oponopono (pronounced *HO-oh-po-no-po-no*) means "to make right" or "to rectify an error." The traditional way to right a wrong required the entire family to attend the healing ritual. With a guide or healer present, each family member had a chance to ask for forgiveness from the others. Morrnah Nalamaku Simeona, kahuna and healer, channeled a new form of Ho'oponopono in which anyone can heal themselves without the formal procedure with the family present.

There is a miraculous story about Dr. Ihaleakala Hew Len, a therapist in Hawaii, who used Ho'oponopono to heal an entire ward of mentally ill criminals. Dr. Hew Len would look over the patient's charts and find himself feeling angry, frustrated, upset, and enraged because these were mentally ill people who committed serious crimes. In some cases, very violent crimes. It's human nature to judge the actions of others, especially when people have done wrong. I also believe that people don't get a chance to heal and be well if they are locked up in prison or in a mental ward. Dr. Hew Len knew he couldn't make the criminals change, but what he did know was that the reality he was experiencing was created through his perception. Dr. Hew Len has said, "If you create your own reality, then you have also created this person, and that person, and the other person too, and me."

The miraculous part of this story was that he didn't try to change his patients. What he focused on instead was healing his perceptions. As a result, slowly but surely, the patients started getting better. Ultimately, they were all healthy and released to be integrated back into society. After four years, the ward closed. This might have been one of those once-in-a-lifetime, miraculous stories, but there's nothing miraculous about the power of forgiveness. When you heal your perceptions, you create your reality, and that heals the environment around you.

I studied psychology in grad school, and what I came to understand was that we can't change people. People have to want to change. And through my own healing journey and spiritual studies, I know that the only thing you can control is yourself and your perceptions. You are 100 percent responsible for your life and how you perceive it. That includes the people around you—they are a part of your creation as well. Once you change your internal world, your external world changes as a result.

There are language, cultural, gender, and generational barriers between me and my father. Speaking to him about my childhood experiences is never going to be met with receptiveness, so I knew I had to do this healing on my own, without his participation. I've had to go on the forgiveness journey without fully expressing to him how much he hurt me. It can be difficult to investigate the most difficult periods of life without involving and communicating with the people who played a part in those experiences. It's particularly difficult if you still have a relationship with someone who has hurt you in the past. But it's completely possible, and even necessary. Be strong, and take this time to begin your journey, knowing that it will take time and effort, but will ultimately be so rewarding.

Ho'oponopono Chant

Listen to and/or chant the ancient Hawaiian prayer Ho'oponopono to usher in a process of healing, forgiveness, love, and transmutation.

This is the short English translation of this prayer:

I am sorry, please forgive me, thank you, I love you.

GO DEEPER

Write a letter to the person/people you want to forgive, including yourself. Keep this letter on your altar until the end of this week (Day 21).

DAY 17
Subconscious Programming

*"Every human brain is both a broadcasting and receiving
station for the vibration of thought ... the subconscious
mind is the 'sending station' of the brain, through which
vibrations of thought are broadcast. The creative imagination
is the 'receiving set,' through which the vibrations of thought
are picked up from the ether."*
—Napoleon Hill, *Think and Grow Rich*

HAVE YOU EVER SEEN the show *The Good Place*? First, it's amazing. Second, there is a particular episode that really nails the importance of subconscious programming. We've done so much to get past the unconscious beliefs that limit us and prevent us from manifesting our desires. But the beliefs we're not consciously aware of can be so hard to get past.

In episode 1 of season 2, the demon Michael erases the memories of main characters Eleanor, Chidi, Tahani, and Jason. No matter how many times Michael gives them different soulmates, environments, and situations, Eleanor and Chidi always figure it out. No matter what Michael tries, they remember their true nature. More specifically, Eleanor and Chidi remember the love between them, because the only real thing that can't be overtaken by environment is love. Your essential being is the same way: you can live anywhere, have any kind of job, surround yourself with any kind of people . . . but you are, ultimately, you. You and the love you have for yourself and your rich, true connections—the ones that are real and soul deep—are the only things that endure when everything else changes.

When we don't take the time to heal the wounds hidden in our subconscious, we're doomed to keep repeating patterns in our lives. But we weren't taught as children to do that kind of work. Instead, we tend to repress what we fear and what we don't want to feel. Later on, as adults, we ask ourselves why we keep manifesting unavailable partners. We ask ourselves, "Why can't I manifest wealth?" The thing is, humans are habitual, and we run on a program dictated by our subconscious mind. For us to disrupt that program, we must look at our subconscious thoughts.

In Dr. Joseph Murphy's book *The Power of Your Subconscious Mind*, he writes that "along with healing, your subconscious darkroom is where your wealth is produced. The key is to first make the subconscious rich before you can see abundance in your life." Our subconscious mind is a system of commands that is at the back burner of our psyche. It dictates the show, though, so it's in our best interest to understand the underlying beliefs that restrict and block our manifestation from coming through. As I mentioned in the first week of this journey, manifesting is our birthright; it should come naturally to us. So, if you aren't manifesting, it's not because you are a bad person: it's because you might be broadcasting the energy of insecurity, scarcity, unworthiness, or just the negativity that accompanies not trusting the process.

Children's brains are pretty much sponges in their environment for the first seven years of their lives. Their brains download information into the subconscious mind to know how to behave, think, and feel in the world. It makes sense, because a child isn't born into this world with a manual for life. To develop belief systems and ways to interact with the world, children observe. Developmental biologist Dr. Bruce Lipton's book *The Biology of Belief* really helps to illustrate the importance of the subconscious mind in early childhood development. He writes, "Since the subconscious mind controls about 95 percent of our behavior, other people essentially program our lives." You may be thinking, *Yikes!* That's how I reacted when I first read this, since I felt it explained so much about my own experience and my worldview. But it's really true: no matter how independent and unique you are, it's true that in those early years, you were inescapably influenced by the people in your world.

I remind you of these facts not to shame you or scare you, but to inform you. Knowledge is power, and knowing the difference between the conscious and subconscious parts of your mind is essential to learning how to navigate the reality of your perception. Our conscious mind is our creative mind. With our conscious mind, we have the capacity to create our reality through our wishes, desires, and what we envision for our lives. You are actively engaging with your conscious mind right now by consciously manifesting something that you desire. By contrast, the subconscious mind works like a computer program. Its commands are automatically activated in response to environmental signals and triggers. Remember *The Good Place* example? This is why toxic positivity is, well, toxic—because no matter how many times you force-feed yourself positivity, whether it's about your life or your ability to manifest or whatever else, your subconscious program will inevitably take over. And if you've experienced adversity as a child, you will feel that no matter what you try to force yourself to think. If you were a refugee, if you experienced homelessness, if your parents went through a bitter divorce, if you were abused or neglected—all of these situations have left your mind and body feeling deeply that the most secure thing to do is revert to old, protective behaviors when the situation is threatening. That can include trying to train yourself to think positively. Even though consciously you may want to be happy, to manifest your desires, to create a new reality—that is scary, and your programming will kick in to "save" you and bring you back to a place that is familiar and, therefore, manageable. So if you have this programming, what do you do?

Our subconscious mind controls 95 percent of our behaviors. That seems daunting, but the good news is that our subconscious minds are also very sensitive to suggestion. You can say all day long "I'm manifesting xyz," but if your subconscious mind is not on board, then you won't manifest it. For some of us, the subconscious programming is so deep that if we say mantras and affirmations like "I am rich," "I am in a soul partnership," they will just be rejected by it. But don't give up! Start with affirmations that your subconscious mind can believe, like "I am becoming more prosperous," or "I am open to love." Once a suggestion sticks, you'll be surprised at the radical transformation that can occur.

Philosophers like René Descartes believed that the mind and body are separate, but now scientists are proving what Eastern practitioners knew all along: that the mind and body are intimately connected in ways we're still uncovering. Thoughts transmitted via the mind's energy directly influence the physical body. Thoughts are energetic vortices that communicate with the cells of the body. This is why I believe it's supremely important to be mindful of what you think about during this manifestation period. Today, take a critical look not just at your own mind, but also what you consume in terms of media—this might constitute messaging that is affecting your subconscious mind in ways you never anticipated. Do a catalog of your reactions to the following lies we're often taught:

★ You have to work hard to be rich.
★ You have to get a college education to make money.
★ "You complete me."
★ Manifestation works for some people but not me.

These are just a few examples of things we may have taken in without even realizing it. Have you internalized any beliefs that are no longer serving you? How can you begin to investigate your subconscious with openness and curiosity?

Curiosity is our gift. When I go on a self-inquiry journey, I ask myself, "What is underneath here?" When I look at the people and situations in my outer realm, I keep in mind that the environment is mirroring something to me that I need to pay attention to. The way to hack the subconscious mind is to only accept universal truths—and question everything else. That way, you can disrupt your subconscious thought patterns by feeding in new ideas and thoughts. With repetition and faith, you can change your outer realm. We live in such an amazing time, when both Western and Eastern spiritual practices are available to us. You can disrupt your programs with a seemingly endless catalog of healing modalities: hypnotherapy, affirmations, embodiment work, energy healing, and more.

Sleep Programming

Right before you fall asleep, when your brain waves are moving more slowly and becoming Delta waves, repeat to yourself one word or a mantra that represents what you are manifesting. Listen to positive affirmations or practice yoga nidra, a form of yoga that induces a deep state of conscious-awareness sleep. This state is deeper than simple relaxation and allows you to be aware of your thoughts.

In the morning, right when you wake up, write morning pages. Morning pages is a practice from Julia Cameron's amazing book *The Artist's Way*. Cameron suggests that you free-write anything that comes up—don't stop or moderate yourself in any way. Essentially, what you're doing while completing morning pages is a form of channeling, or downloading. As Dr. Joseph Murphy writes in *The Power of*

Your Subconscious Mind, just before sleep or right after waking up in the morning is the best time to imprint new associations onto your subconscious mind. It's a powerful kind of preliminary manifestation that can be very enlightening.

GO DEEPER

Seek an embodiment coach, a professional who can work with you to find new lifestyle techniques that are in line with your unique body. Today is a perfect day to try tapping, energy healing, or any other modalities that can help you access your subconscious mind.

DAY 18
Shadow Work

"Everyone carries a shadow, and the less it is embodied in the individual's conscious life, the blacker and denser it is. . . . At all counts, it forms an unconscious snag, thwarting our most well-meant intentions."
—Carl Jung

YESTERDAY, WE TALKED about the subconscious mind and how it defaults to certain programming even when we're not aware of it. Today, we will dive deeper into that unknown with shadow work. You might have heard about shadow work. Actually, the most popular question I get asked these days is "What is shadow work?" It is an essential part of the journey into understanding the root cause of your blocks.

I decided to declare my major in college after a psychology class in which I learned about Carl Jung. Jung, a Swiss psychologist, developed a number of influential concepts that continue to be part of the language of self-exploration today, including the "shadow self," which is the basis for what we call shadow work. Jung believed that everyone has a shadow aspect, and integrating it into your conscious personality is so important because it can be helpful in terms of getting past obstacles. Sometimes it is more useful than any other kind of healing, particularly if you have experienced trauma.

Jung termed the shadow as the aspect of an individual's personality, often deemed as unsavory or unacceptable, which then gets repressed into the hidden parts of the human psyche. The shadow aspect is what society, our culture, or our family deems as taboo. This can be sexual desire, career aspiration, gender presentation, or any number of things that might go against the perceived norm in your world. Jung wrote that when we express these parts of ourselves, we feel shame, so we repress them. He suggests that the more you repress these desires, feelings, and urges, the more often they are projected into your experiences.

For my own part, I didn't get to pursue my artistic career in college, and so my artistic endeavors took a back burner to "making it." As a result, I repressed my creativity. This neglected aspect of myself became my shadow. Because I didn't have a healthy way of expressing myself, that repression turned to addiction. Whenever I would meet someone who was in a creative field, it would trigger all of these negative feelings such as jealousy and anger. Today, think about what shadow aspects you might have repressed, and how these behaviors might be finding their way into your daily life now. If you can pinpoint this process before it takes hold and instead turn toward your shadow with compassion and give yourself space to be your true self, you can head off unhealthy behaviors and patterns of thought before they begin. This is why the process of identifying your shadow, doing shadow work, and then integrating your shadow is so important. When we individuate—another term coined by Carl Jung, representing the journey a mind must undergo to achieve wholeness— we manifest ourselves.

The ego works in binaries—light and dark, good and bad—but spirituality and the Divine don't distinguish between these qualities. All are part of the whole. Carl Jung also understood that the shadow cannot be destroyed, and repression of or the failure to acknowledge and integrate the shadow leads to projection. The author of the blog *Arts of Thought* wrote that projection "serves as a defense mechanism which temporarily alleviates someone from the pains of facing their own shadow." The strong and often unconscious desire to avoid pain makes stopping projection impossible, so if there's a trait of ours that we've been pushing down into our unconscious, it's inevitable that it will bubble up into our behaviors and thoughts.

For example, when someone is on the journey of manifesting a life partner or a divine counterpart, understanding the shadow and the act of projection is a pretty important step. If the shadow goes unchecked, people can attract their partner from their shadow. For example, someone with abandonment wounds can attract someone who is co-dependent, or they themselves will push others away with their co-dependent behaviors.

There are four basic steps in Jungian shadow work

1. Accept the truth that our shadow traits cannot be repressed out of existence.
2. Take time for introspection and accept the root of each shadow trait.
3. Work to bring aspects of these shadow traits into the light.
4. Allow shadow traits to express themselves in healthy ways.

The unconscious mind can be accessed through meditation, psychotherapy, active introspection, or dream work. People have even used psychedelics to reach what Jung called "the Unconscious Conscious."

But shadow work includes the word *work* for a reason—because it's something that you *do* as opposed to just read about. Our shadows aren't bad, per se; it's just that we've deemed them unworthy or bad and pushed them down below the surface. It takes time and effort to bring these parts of ourselves back to the surface, and it can be hard and painful.

Often, we look back at our lives and realize that we could have saved ourselves from a lot of pain if we had just looked at our fears and limiting beliefs instead of running away from them, because they all catch up with us anyway in some way or another. Author Brené Brown has written that our first response to fear is often to numb ourselves to make it go away. We don't lean in; we run away. And as she says, one of the most popular ways of numbing ourselves in modern life is by being busy: "living so hard and fast that the truths of our lives can't catch up with us . . . We fill every ounce of white space with something so there's no room or time for emotion to make itself known." Is this something you are doing in your own life?

If you don't know how to give yourself the space to be real with your emotions, now is the time to do the work. Don't internalize when you're met with negativity, heartbreak, and regret. Give yourself the time to mourn and heal from your wounds, and be honest about who you are and the choices you've made.

When we feel triggered, it is a wound that is reflected to us by someone or something else. When we feel jealous or competitive, or we compare ourselves to someone, it's an inner reflection of something that our heart truly desires. Shadow work is being aware of these feelings so that you don't project your wounds onto something or someone else. It's also about expanding your awareness, which is essential for manifesting the things that you want most deeply—and not inadvertently calling the wrong things into the world, whether those are deeply damaging relationships, false goals, or other visions that seem positive but are only projections of your own illusory and incomplete self.

One of my moon circle members mentioned that bringing up the shadow to the level of the conscious mind is incredibly uncomfortable because it's all the content that you've hidden away. This process is inherently unsettling, but when you go through it, you reclaim parts of yourself that you were missing. And by reclaiming your missing parts, you can be surer of your desires, and more able to bring them into being.

Shadow Work

Review the four steps of Jungian shadow work, and then use the thoughts that surface to do a little active introspection and journaling. Here are some questions you can use as prompts:

★ What parts of you have you abandoned?
★ What have you repressed?
★ What do you hide in the shadow because you thought it was bad?

GO DEEPER

Use a tarot or oracle deck to give yourself a reading. I particularly like Kim Krans's *Wild Unknown Archetypes* deck, which is perfect for shadow work. I love this deck. It has helped me so much in my healing journey and understanding the archetypes in my own psyche.

DAY 19
Fear Setting

"Never say never, because limits, like fears,
are often just an illusion."
—Michael Jordan, NBA Hall of Fame induction speech

TODAY WE WILL CONTINUE to turn toward our anxieties instead of running away. Give yourself a moment of grace for continuing on this journey in spite of the discomfort you may feel. Remember that you are ultimately treating yourself with kindness by opening yourself up to the possibility of successful manifestation—so keep that in mind as we talk about another potentially painful subject today: fear.

Writing a book has always been on my list of things I wanted to manifest, but when I finally got the offer, I was crippled with fear. I'm the first person in my family who is a published author, a daughter of immigrants whose first language is not English. My parents learned English in school, but just as many English-speaking Americans learn Spanish in school, it's a whole other story when you have to speak a second language fluently. My parents did not go to college in America. When they immigrated, they learned English by living here—a crash course in immersive learning. They watched television and learned along the way. Pretty badass if you ask me.

When my family moved to the suburbs of New York, I started first grade in a new school, and they put me in ESL (English as a second language). Granted, English was not my first language, but they assumed I didn't speak English fluently based on my ethnicity. The teachers eventually realized that I could speak English so they quickly pulled me out of ESL. This mistake on the part of an administration happened because they made assumptions about me. But, because by then I had heard from teachers that I was not proficient in the English language, that fact imprinted on my mind. I extended this belief to my parents, who speak English with an Asian accent and have trouble pronouncing words like *capacity*. God bless them.

I had to work through my fears and doubts about my fluency in English. Going into academia helped. Having to write a lengthy research paper for my master's thesis definitely helped. Having a blog for over ten years helped. Being a voracious reader certainly helped. You will never be fearless, because fear is a necessary and natural feeling. The way to overcome it is by doing.

When my clients are crippled by anxiety and cannot seem to take action, I ask them to either tell me all their fears or write them down. I want to know what they are so afraid of and why. I learned this practice from author Tim Ferris. Instead of goal setting, he recommends fear setting—moving toward your fears instead of away from them. I found this practice to be incredibly helpful, because our minds trick us sometimes. As we have explored on this journey, human beings are more comfortable with the known than the unknown. The reptilian part of our brain looks out for threatening circumstances and keeps us ready to retreat even if what we are doing means we are moving closer to our dreams. We have to be extra vigilant with our conscious minds so that we notice a reptilian response that might derail us as we get closer to bringing our desires into reality.

So to fear set, you write down your greatest fears and worst-case scenarios, as well as your backup plans. Once you write them down, you'll notice that they'll immediately begin to seem less daunting, and often you'll realize right away how irrational they are. You will soon accept there is nothing to be afraid of. Fear setting is a great way to prove to yourself just how often your ego will tell you all the different reasons why some-thing will go wrong when it's just not true.

Fear holds us back from taking action because we are afraid of what other people might think. We believe that if we fail, being judged will prevent us from moving forward with our idea. I don't believe that we can be fearless. But we have an amygdala, which is the part of the brain where the response to fear is initiated. And while we need the amyg-dala, because we do need to respond to dangerous stimuli, it's possible for us to ignore the fear responses it sends us. We can choose to meet our fears and try to investigate the content behind them. Next time you feel threatened or like you can't do the thing you want, ask yourself why you are afraid. What is the root cause?

You will have to distinguish between what is a genuine fear—like the desire to run for your life if there's a *Revenant* bear situation going down—as opposed to fearful content in your mind that's not real, like a perception that others will judge you for launching a business venture and failing. To do this, you will need to become really comfortable with your fear. You've heard that saying "Get comfortable in the discomfort," and it really applies here, because any type of growth or manifestation process will require you to take risks and move beyond your fears, even if it scares you.

Another popular saying is that nothing good comes from your comfort zone. I try to do something that terrifies me each year just so I don't get too comfortable, and I recommend you try it too! If you feel like you're in a rut, do something that is scary as hell to get the juices flowing again. One year, I learned how to scuba dive, because do you *really* want to know how vast and deep the oceans are? Maybe not, but I felt like a better person after I opened myself up to that knowledge. I've gone sky diving, asked a hot life-guard if I could sit with him on his lifeguard tower, went skinny dipping in the ocean, did my first Instagram live in 2018 and talked about spirituality, quit my corporate job. Think about what makes you stop in your tracks and struggle not to run in the opposite direction. Then do that thing!

You want to manifest from your higher self, not from a wounded ego. I believe that when we make a decision and we have an intention, and it is in alignment with our values and serves the greater humanity, the Universe unfolds for us and sends to us the right opportunities, people, ideas, and resources to channel the energy through Spirit.

The ego is the most fearful part of us. It's that little voice inside of our heads that tells us that we're not good, beautiful, smart, or skinny enough. When we listen to this little voice, it prevents us from taking action and putting ourselves out there. A huge part of manifestation is deciding and taking the necessary action steps toward our goals. We have free will and we need to match the Universe in all the gifts that are in store for us.

When we criticize ourselves, or we feel rejected, our wounded ego will create stories in our head about who we are. These stories hold us back from moving on. The voice you hear is the conditioned part of you that is fearful and wants to remain small in the name of protection. It sees you as a victim of your circumstances. Love that part of you. Call back the pieces of you that you've lost. Remember that this part of you only knows fear. Our ego is necessary because it protects us, but when we allow it to lead our lives, we operate from a broken place. We have to look outside of ourselves to feel whole and to manifest.

Fear Setting

Write all your fears down on a piece of paper. Which fears are you ready to release? Place this on paper on your altar until Day 21.

GO DEEPER

Do something today that you are afraid of. Ask someone out on a date. Do an Instagram Live. Create a video about something you love. Swim in the ocean.

DAY 20
Healing the Past

"Healing is an art. It takes time, it takes practice.
It takes love."
—Maza Dohta

DAY 20 IS ALL ABOUT HEALING. As we've explored before, healing your beliefs and perceptions is what will lead you to co-create with the Universe, and it's a crucial part of the manifestation process. As you began moving through this world, you started to forget who you really are. Our collective amnesia, our collective disconnection with the Divine, strips down our defenses and eats away at our strength. Healing is the process of remembering and re-arming yourself after years of loss. Just as a reminder, you don't have to be healed to receive your blessing. We embark on a healing journey not because we are damaged and broken, but to become closer to our soul, our true nature.

I mentioned it before and I'll mention it again: healing is not linear. I see it as a spiral. I also see it as the ebbs and flows of life. Something might come back to trigger you that you thought you had already healed, but it might have come back in a different form. One thing to remember here is that you have more knowledge, experience, and wisdom this time around than when you did when you were first wounded. You are never at the same point on your healing journey, even if some days it might feel that way.

The reason why so many of us "fail" at manifesting is because we are still carrying our own trauma and wounds from our past, as well as the intergenerational trauma carried by our ancestors.

Han (한) is a Korean word that indicates an intrinsic, visceral, gut feeling saturated with centuries of oppression, sorrow, anger, rage, and resentment—it includes the feelings of injustice that the Korean people and diaspora deeply feel and share. It is a word and response rooted in Korea's history, past and present, of foreign oppression and pain. You might be reading this and asking, "What does that have to do with manifesting?" The answer is that I believe many people can't manifest, or they give up on their manifestation journey, because it's not as simple as "change your thoughts, change your life"—even though so many manifestation teachings put it just that simply. There's more to it than that. It's also about healing our intergenerational trauma surrounding the feelings of safety and security. The failure to manifest is so often met with shame and guilt—people think they are doing it wrong—but the fact is that it might not just be about your personal efforts.

Milagros Phillips, a race healer and a guest on my podcast, says that you need two things to heal: (1) history and (2) being trauma-informed. We can only heal what we know and understand, and understanding our history, as well as our ancestral trauma, will help us understand our own limiting beliefs and blocks. We can't change what we don't know and what we don't understand.

As on Day 15, when we honored our past, today we should take the time to investigate the wounds that go back to our parents, our parents' parents, and beyond. When we understand what happened in the past, we gain so much knowledge to work with today. Milagros uses storytelling as a way to educate people on racism. She believes that we need to heal before transformation can take place. As the late novelist Michael Crichton allegedly said, "If you don't know history, then you don't know anything. You are a leaf that doesn't know it is part of a tree."

I've seen it within my own parents. My dad is the embodiment of a scarcity mentality. Everything he does is with the goal of saving money. So many of my parents' fights were about money, or lack thereof, or how to spend it. I grew up with the mindset that money equaled conflict. He would get upset with me on a regular basis because I was "wasting" money. I didn't understand why he was like that until I found out that his parents struggled with money. They also lived with a constant fear for their physical safety. My grandparents came of age during the Japanese colonial rule in Korea, when women were in danger of becoming comfort women for the Japanese military. Koreans were stripped of their livelihood, their spiritual practices, their land, and their freedom. By the time my grandparents had my dad, who was born in 1949, it was the year before the Korean War. They were a family of eight, barely making ends meet, and things were very tough while he was growing up, as the country was split in two. Sometimes, my dad will share his story when I ask him about his experiences living during that period, but it still triggers him, and he usually responds with anger and sadness. His parents (my grandparents) always fought over money and distributing resources among the children. Especially during the Korean War, when they barely had enough food to feed all six children, their goal every day was to survive.

The opposite of my father, my mom grew up in a wealthy household. My grandfather was an entrepreneur, and she grew up feeling secure in money, food, and her basic needs being met. My dad, being one of six children, always struggled. He grew up with the mentality of "there is not enough." My dad always talks about how poor his family was and how there wasn't enough food to go around. As a result, I grew up with a lot of mixed messages. My mom told me not to worry about money and then my dad told me there was never enough. My dad said that he had everything except money, and I think over the years, my dad's mentality rubbed off on my mom. She has always instilled in me that you can be anything you want to be. But after years of my dad repeating his warning, she began to add a note of caution to her advice. My way of seeing the world—my creativity and nonconformism—was "fine" . . . that is, until I quit my corporate job. And for my part, my initial response was to panic when I found I had to take full responsibility of my finances. Unless you're "in" it, you don't realize what that kind of responsibility entails. This was the year of the Girl Boss movement and Me Too, a time when female empowerment was exercised by women leaving their patriarchal jobs and starting their own ventures. The reality of it wasn't as simple as they made it seem to be. When I didn't get that steady paycheck from "the man," and the veil was lifted off the romanticized version of entrepreneurship, I realized I had to do a whole other level of spiritual work. I truly believe entrepreneurship is a spiritual journey because you constantly have to negotiate with your ego, be consistent, and make sure you're seen and valued. You have to launch yourself out into the abyss of this world.

I have compassion for my dad and my grandparents, as I'm sure it was not easy for them to feel abundant when their country was being torn apart and their only concern was survival. I feel compassion for my mom, who was influenced by my dad and wanted security and success for me. And finally, I feel compassion for myself, because I had only the information available to me at the time I was growing up to begin to make decisions about what I would do with my life and how I would feel safe and secure. We are all products of our environments, and we do the best we can with what we have.

One thing you will see over and over again when you read about trauma is that if we don't learn to regulate our nervous systems, we will always be triggered by our environment. During my doctorate program, I realized that in psychology there was a missing focus on the body, its energy, and the spiritual aspect of humans. Understanding things at an intellectual level, in my experience, does not heal trauma. What does? Having mindfulness practices that help you regulate your nervous system—and obviously policy changes that dismantle oppressive systems. The feeling of scarcity is a visceral root chakra trigger. At the beginning of the pandemic, all I heard about on the news was people buying toilet paper. That's easy to understand in the context of trauma: when people are afraid, they can only think about their basic survival needs. They were also acting on their fear of scarcity. The healing work that I do is informed by Resmaa Menakem's work and his book *My Grandmother's Hands: Racialized Trauma and the Pathway to Mending Our Hearts and Bodies.* In his book, he shares historical contexts of the trauma experienced in white-bodied folks and people of color. The author offers body practices to heal our bodies of trauma since it lives in our bodies—I highly recommend reading this book.

As much as I'm an advocate of talk therapy, from my own experience, no matter how much I talked about my past, I just never seemed to be able to move on from it. Seeing a therapist helped me to talk about my life with an objective person, someone who wasn't a part of it. I felt very deeply that I was missing a key component of my healing journey, and that was a more spiritual approach. There's a quote from the book *The Celestine Prophecy* written by James Redfield that illustrates this same sentiment. It's difficult to move beyond deep emotional hurts by just talking about the past, but people can transcend by tuning in to the divine part of themselves—as Redfield describes it, "their very own Spiritual Consciousness, not just a religious belief." This is further acknowledgment that what has happened in the past is a key component of your journey now. As we've noted before, you have to let those old parts of you die—metaphorically, of course—to create your new reality.

Healing is not always comfortable, and it can be tough; it's a continuous journey. It can be exhausting. On the bright side, the more layers you peel away, the more liberated you will feel. Not only did I have to understand my ancestors' history, my parents' experience as immigrants while I was growing up, and my own experience being Korean American, I also had to take a critical look at how I view scarcity versus abundance. The biggest challenge of all was being able to have confidence in myself that I could make money doing what I loved. And that took healing my programming around what it would take to create a life that I love, doing what feels aligned, and knowing that I would be taken care of financially. I would call this entire process, including the crucial healing component, manifestation.

If you are on a similar journey healing your parents' negative beliefs around success, money, or living your truth when it doesn't correspond to the "norm," then you may be facing an intense struggle. And even if you get to the place where you can manifest the reality you want, you may fear for the family you might feel you've left behind. To this day, I still fear that my parents will never enjoy their lives because they've equated the American Dream with punishingly hard work. But by now, I know I can't change my parents. What I can heal is my lineage. When I live differently, I am infusing my epigenetic line with rest, joy, and pleasure. You can do that too for the people who have cared for you, even if you feel that you are no longer have the same values as they do. Epigenetics is an emerging scientific field that studies, as the National Human Genome Research Institute puts it, "heritable changes caused by the activation and deactivation of genes without any change in the underlying DNA sequence of the organism." What this means for us is that when our grandparents or great-grandparents (or ancestors even further back in our family line) experienced a trauma, if they didn't fully process and resolve or release that experience, it created what we call epigenetic markers on DNA. These markers get passed down from generation to generation.

I believe scarcity mentality is passed down from generation to generation. Just as genes get passed down from your ancestors, so does trauma. If your ancestors have always been oppressed and struggling, chances are your genes are activating the feeling of scarcity. I started to do the work by doing ancestral healing, decolonization work, and connecting with my ancestors on the other side. I encourage you to learn more about the motivations of your family and your ancestors. It's an ongoing journey of learning and unlearning. And I believe that if you are here today, your ancestors are helping you break the intergenerational traumas and recode your epigenetic DNA with rest and abundance.

As I've said before, your healing journey will be that much more fulfilling if you focus on healing your perceptions rather than trying to change the world around you. Which is why during this journey we will talk about healing your belief in scarcity in many different ways. You are learning to see the world and your role in it in a new light. And as a result, you will begin to understand that you are the creator of your universe, and with that power, you hold a certain responsibility.

The point of healing is not to be perfect; it's to be well again. Kintsugi is the Japanese art of repairing broken pieces of pottery with lacquered gold. As a Zen Buddhist philosophy, Kintsugi is about embracing the flawed and imperfect. It's such a beautiful metaphor for us as humans. The gold highlights the cracks in the pottery, which, to me, only makes it more beautiful. Just like in humans, you might think your cracks make you damaged, but they make you who you are: beautiful, nuanced, complex, and worthy. Healing allows us to navigate through the imperfectly perfect reality of life. Healing will allow you to trust again that something good will inevitably happen to you.

Self-Healing

Do something healing for yourself. Take a bath, listen to beautiful music, make comforting food, talk to a friend, watch your favorite movie, or snuggle your pet. I've learned that resting is a form of healing intergenerational trauma. If your ancestors were colonized or oppressed, chances are they never rested. Resting also helps us tap into our creativity—consider taking some time of relaxation and doing something creative and expressive, like painting, crafting, singing, or dancing.

GO DEEPER

Ancestral Healing

If your parents are still with you and you feel open and called, ask them the following questions:

1. How did you grow up? What was happening around you at the time?
2. What were your parents' views on money, scarcity, and abundance? Was money tight?
3. How did your parents get along? Did they ever argue about money?
4. What were your parents' dreams? Did your parents pursue their dreams?
5. What was your life like before I came along?

You can take it a step further and research online what was happening in the news at the time when your parents were children, and when they were coming of age.

If your grandparents are still alive, you can ask them the same questions. If you have a connection to your ancestors on the other side, go into meditation and ask them.

DAY 21
Release Ritual

"When I let go of what I am, I become what I might be.
When I let go of what I have, I receive what I need."
—Lao Tzu, *Tao Te Ching*

RITUALS ARE WAYS TO MARK the passage of time and to bring spiritual significance to important acts. Blowing out your candles on your birthday is a ritual to bring in blessings and good wishes for your solar return. Graduation signifies an ending to your studies, and at the same time, there is a commencement speech—*commencement* means "a new beginning." There are so many different types of rituals in life, even secular life, that solidify an ending and simultaneously call in a new beginning. Today, the twenty-first day of our journey, is an important day to close one chapter of your old self. Today is the day to let go of the parts of you that are no longer in alignment with the version of you that you're manifesting. This ritual will also help prepare for all the things you are calling into your life.

First, I'll introduce some principles that will allow you to promote the flow of energy. If you've watched *Tidying Up with Marie Kondo* on Netflix or you understand the principles around feng shui (pronounced "fung shwee"), you know that there is an energetic release when you clear your space. In Reiki, I always tell my students that the best way to have energy flowing to you is to clear the clutter from your physical space. This energy is called chi (pronounced "chee"). We need to make room for the thing that we are bringing in before we call for it.

As I'm writing this book right now, I am two months away from a milestone birthday. When this book is published, I will be forty years old. During the last year of my thirties, it was all about releasing the past. The biggest thing I wanted to release this year was the need for validation. I wanted so badly to be seen by my family and friends. But I had to own that my path is different from the people around me, my culture, my family, and my friends. I had to acknowledge that nobody is going to understand me and my motivations completely, and that's okay. I don't have one word to describe what I do for a living. I didn't take a linear path. Currently, I'm single and have no children. I've never been married or had a mortgage. I used to feel a certain way about this, and I think holding on to that need was blocking me from so many blessings that were meant for me. Writing this book has been so cathartic. Sharing my story feels so aligned, and when I step into things that make me feel like this, the Universe says, "Hey, she likes this! Let's bring more of this to her!" As I approach forty, I'm proud of myself for taking the road less traveled. I'm proud to have stood up for myself so I could break away from the norm, because now I get to share my experiences with you.

I encourage you to take this time to acknowledge the path you have taken and to celebrate it, even if it's not the narrative you might have written for yourself when you began. If you are not the "norm"— great! It's even more evidence that you have chosen to be who you are in spite of all the pressure to change, to repress, to deny. You are not your environment, your family, or your friends. You are you, and you have the power to cast off the limiting beliefs that could be keeping you from realizing your manifestations.

Today is a sacred time to create a ritual around all the things you wrote down over the last few days. You now have physical representations of your limiting beliefs, fears, and shadows and you know who you are forgiving. You have also made steps to honor and begin to understand your past. Just know that deep inside, all these experiences and lessons will always be a part of you, but this ritual is your vow to not live in them anymore. You are letting these things go, extracting the wisdom that you've learned and moving forward. *Transmutation* means "changing or altering matter in form, appearance, or nature" and especially indicates a transformation to a higher form. Today, imagine all the things you've written down being transmuted into energy that will be rebirthed into a new you.

I commend you for making it through this week. Your healing journey will continue after this forty-day journey is over, and for the rest of your life. There is nothing more rewarding than healing your mind, body, and soul. And releasing your old story that bound you to the past and creating a different future for yourself is extremely cathartic. Take the time to feel joy and sit with the freedom that you now have. You have cut the cords of what was tethering you to negative emotions and experiences and now you can manifest from a different place—a more whole one.

Release Ritual

Gather all the papers on which you wrote your fears this week. Over a fire or in a cauldron, burn them all. Say a prayer of your choice. I recommend asking Mother Earth to help you transmute these negative energies. Imagine white light encompassing the things you've burned. You're free!

GO DEEPER

It may seem simple, but clean your physical space. Donate or throw away what you don't need. Read Marie Kondo's book *The Life-Changing Magic of Tidying Up: The Japanese Art of Decluttering and Organizing,* which is based on the KonMari Method. Alternatively, watch her Netflix series.

I consulted a feng shui practitioner in 2009. For context, I was living with my parents and just newly single. She told me to clean my room, get rid of anything with "old" energies, buy a new queen-size bed (big enough to accommodate a partner), and set an intention that I was open and ready for love. I did everything she told me to do, and within five months, I moved in with my new boyfriend. I'm not saying that this was the only thing that helped me to manifest, because it wasn't, but it was a huge contributor to my success. Maybe my story will entice you to work with a feng shui expert.

Week 4

DAYS 22-28

The Energetic Shift

Everything is energy: love and money, time and action.
In Week 4, we'll not only investigate the energies that
move our lives and motivate our actions but also learn
how to optimize them for the purposes of manifestation.
That includes chakra work, developing affirmations and
mantras, scripting new narratives for the future, and
other useful techniques that will allow you to be in the
flow and receive.

DAY 22
Chakras

"Everything is energy and that's all there is to it.
Match the frequency of the reality you want and you
cannot help but get that reality. It can be no other way.
This is not philosophy. This is physics."
—Darryl Anka

YOU'VE MADE IT through twenty-one days. I'm so proud of you! The past week may have been painful, but you've begun the work of understanding yourself and healing your wounds, including generational trauma. I encourage you to continue on the path of healing, which is nonlinear and unending. But in terms of concentrating your efforts during this forty-day journey to manifesting your new reality, this week is all about energy. We'll start to create the energetic shifts from within that will help us move toward our new identity and vibrate at a higher frequency. You are getting closer to your soul, the energetic signature beyond your old stories, and the key to understanding the new ones you are writing now.

We've discussed how being in the present moment and noticing signs and synchronicities is such an important part of the manifestation process. The next step is developing the ability to discern when to take action.

And discernment is a quality that is built on trust—trusting yourself when you feel that your desire means something.

When I quit my job in 2017, I started traveling the world. While I hoped to be a travel blogger/writer/photographer, to be honest, I wasn't quite sure if that was my purpose. I just decided to take that path because I really loved it. I believed that when you do something you love, it will never lead you astray. So when I had the opportunity to go on a sailing trip to Mallorca, Spain, in June 2018, during the summer solstice, I jumped to do it. If you were wondering—no, I didn't intentionally manifest the trip, but I felt that it came at the perfect time. I considered myself to be at the apex of where I wanted to be, and I felt that it was an unexpected manifestation from the Universe.

Everyone on the trip was wonderful. There were no egos, and everyone wanted to be there to capture the beauty of Mallorca. It was one of the most memorable trips I've ever been on, and I was sailing with almost twenty complete strangers. Even though we were still getting to know one another, I felt especially connected to some of my fellow travelers. I spent the evening of the summer solstice watching the sunset from the boat. I found myself talking to a yoga teacher and Reiki healer named Michelle. As she was gazing into the orange sun, all of a sudden she turned toward me and whispered, "Have you ever considered doing energy healing or working with crystals?" In my conscious mind, I didn't know what she was talking about and felt like it kind of came out of nowhere. But somewhere in my soul, there was recognition. To this day, Michelle doesn't remember this exchange at all, but we both believe in signs coming from the Divine— and this was definitely a sign.

I went back home to New York and a week later, I was enrolled in a class on Reiki levels 1 and 2. I wasn't quite sure where this journey was going to lead me, but I knew in my gut that I was going in the right direction. Reiki 1 was absolutely the beginning of my healing journey—it affected me that much. Reiki unearths the things that have happened in your life, which might be buried deep in your body and subconscious. Even if you don't have the words to articulate what you are feeling, the emphasis on energy healing and psychosomatic responses are an amazing way to help you process emotions that may be stuck.

During that first course, I discovered that my Reiki master was also a Kundalini yoga teacher. She encouraged me to study more about energy through Kundalini yoga, and that felt right too. After doing some initial study in Kundalini, I found that I felt even better and lighter, so I committed to learning more. Four months later, I was in Rishikesh, India, studying with a guru. Just to be clear, I'm not telling you to pick up your life and move to India. What I am saying, however, is that when you get a sign and it doesn't make sense to you in your logical mind, sometimes your soul just knows, so you just have to *do*.

So often, the Universe will leave you a trail of breadcrumbs, and today is about following them. It's also specifically about energy, how it flows in your body and around you. Understanding energy is crucial to understanding life. Everything is energy. When you're manifesting, you're working with energy. Energy cannot be contained; it moves through us. You must learn to flow with energy.

If you're manifesting money, you have to understand that money moves through us; it is an exchange. And money is manifested through other people. People pay us because we've set a value on our work, goods, or services, and in exchange for that, we receive money. The concept of money has become distorted, because we've attached meaning to it. We associate our state of being to it. We equate our sense of worth with the amount of money we have. This is also based on our own personal definition of wealth. So if you look at your bank account and you always feel like there's never enough, you might feel like you're not enough. To heal your money mindset, remember that money is just energy—it isn't inherently good or bad, and whether you have it or not does not affect who you are.

One of my teachers told me that it's much easier to shift energy than it is to move matter. And matter is just energy particles that are densely packed together. Everything in the Universe is made up of atoms. Quantum physics is the study of matter and energy at the fundamental level. Quantum physicists have said that when you look at atoms at their most subatomic form, they're just waves of energy. Modern-day scientists are confirming what the rishis, yogis, and sages have always known, that we too are energy. Deepak Chopra has said, "Quantum physics has found that there is no empty space in the human cell, but it is a teeming, electric-magnetic field of possibility or potential." We are literally energetic beings. When I learned this, it made everything seem possible.

In Daniel Reid's book *The Complete Book of Chinese Health and Healing,* he writes, "Taoists have known about the earth's electromagnetic field for at least 5,000 years. Chee-gung ('energy work') tunes the frequency of human energy with that of the earth." Because everything in the universe is made of energy, humans are affected by the gravitational pulls of the celestial bodies, Earth, and each other. For example, the twenty-eight-day menstrual cycle of a female is synced to the cyclical phases of the moon and Earth's magnetic field. A full moon has the ability to rise the tides of the oceans that cover 75 percent of Earth's surface, and since human bodies are made of up 75 percent water, we are affected energetically.

The content that I learned during my Reiki trainings and Kundalini yoga teacher training confirmed the statement that "Everything you need is within you." It sounds so simple, but so many different healing modalities back it up. You really can shift your outer reality with your breath, mind, and energy. And while I'm simplifying this concept—because there are eight limbs of yoga, and therefore more nuance and more wisdom if you dive in and commit to study—it's true that the more you practice, the more you start to shift. The environment around you begins to change, and then the process gathers momentum and you start to believe. To me, this is alchemy.

Tech guru Steve Jobs's favorite book was said to be *The Autobiography of a Yogi* by Paramahansa Yogananda. There are many reasons why Jobs might have favored this book, but I believe reading it gave Jobs insight into how to move his body to open up his energy centers, which allowed him to be in the creative flow. As you know, Steve Jobs was able to create and invent things ahead of his time. I remember when the iPod came out, and then the iPhone—it seemed like he had an unending capacity for technological marvels.

Yogis call this energy *Kundalini*, or "life force energy." This is the latent energy that lives at the base of our spine. In Sanskrit, *kundal* translates to "coil" and *kundalini* comes from *kunda*, which means "deeper place, pit, or cavity." Therefore, as Swami Satyananda Saraswati writes in his book *Kundalini Tantra*, "Kundalini refers to the shakti or power when it is in its dormant potential state, but when it is manifesting, you can call it Devi, Kali, Durga, Saraswati, Lakshmi, or any other name according to the manifestation it is exhibiting before you." I believe we all have a creative potential that lies within us. The energy lies there, dormant, until we wake it up or activate it. First, we must have awareness that we have this potential energy and then we can use it to unleash the dormant creative potential within us, and therefore, manifest. Then you will realize that everything really is truly within you.

Kundalini is just one example of an energy that exists in your body, and I include it because it is a system I've learned, but there are many other practices and modalities that aim toward the same thing, which is to awaken this creative potential. With focused attention, breath, movement, and visualization, you can move latent energy up into your centers, called chakras. By understanding each one, you can balance and improve the energy flow in your body.

Chakra in Sanskrit means "wheel of energy." I am going to mention seven chakras here, but we have many more than that. And while there are discrepancies among different texts when it comes to the colors of the chakras, I'm going to use the ones that my teacher taught me. Keep in mind that this is a very basic description of the chakras. I encourage you to read more about the chakras and yoga, especially from teachers whose indigeneity is from the part of the world where these theories originated. Some of you may be familiar with American psychologist Abraham Maslow and his hierarchy of needs. I learned that when he was developing his theory, he was influenced by the chakra system. Both systems speak to our needs in a given area of our lives, whether spiritual, emotional, or psychological, that must be fulfilled in order for us to reach self-actualization and enlightenment.

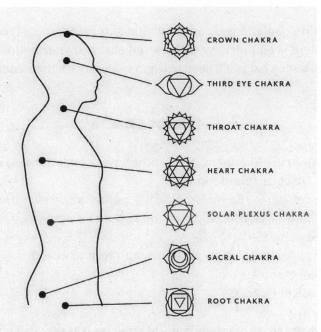

CROWN CHAKRA

THIRD EYE CHAKRA

THROAT CHAKRA

HEART CHAKRA

SOLAR PLEXUS CHAKRA

SACRAL CHAKRA

ROOT CHAKRA

Prāna, the Sanskrit word for "vital principle," refers to what is called the "subtle body"—the part of being that is not entirely physical, nor completely spiritual. It can mean breath, life force, or universal energy. Pranayam (*prāna* + *āyāma*, or "to lengthen or extend") is one of the eight limbs of yoga. And, true to its literal translation, it is the practice of extending breath, extending life force energy.

According to yoga philosophy, prana flows through the nadis, or energetic channels. There are said to be seventy-two thousand nadis in the subtle body. If you are more familiar with Traditional Chinese Medicine, nadis are similar to energy meridians, and prana is qi or chi. There are three main nadis: the ida, pingala, and sushumna. The ida nadi is the left, lunar, yin channel. The pingala is the right, solar, yang channel. The sushumna nadi is the main energy channel that flows with the spinal cord. The ida and pingala weave through the chakras like a DNA helix. The chakras start at the root, the Muladhara, and extend up to the crown, the Sahasrara chakra. Each chakra has a different vibrational frequency:

it has a unique energetic, elemental, auditory, emotional, and physical focus. Here is an overview of the seven chakras, an introduction to provide you with what you'll need to begin to work with their energies.

1. Root Chakra

Sanskrit: Mūlādhāra; *mul* (sometimes spelled mool) means "root or foundation"
Location: In the male body, the perineum, and in the female body, the posterior of the cervix
Element: Earth
Traditional Symbology: Lotus with four deep-crimson petals
Beej Mantra: Lam
Musical Note: C

Without our sense of grounding and security, it is very difficult to access our creative energy. When our bodies are in a state of survival, we are not open to the infinite possibilities. I don't want to categorize the order of importance on the chakras, because they are all integral to your whole being, but the root is especially important in the context of this journey because it is how we manifest through the physical plane. Think of the roots of the tree. Without nourishment, the roots of a grand oak tree would die. In Maslow's hierarchy of needs, the root chakra would signify basic human needs such as shelter, food, and water. One question to ask yourself as you work with the root chakra is, "Do I feel safe?"

2. Sacral Chakra

Sanskrit: Svādhiṣṭhāna; *sva* means "one's own" and *adhisthana* means "dwelling place or residence"
Location: Base of the spine

Element: Water
Traditional Symbology: Lotus with six red-orange petals
Beej Mantra: Vam
Musical Note: D

This is the center that holds our sexual energies: the feminine and masculine. These are our primal energies and they can be harnessed in a variety of different ways. On the physical level, this can be expended through sex, and one of the ways in which this energy can manifest is a baby. On the emotional level, it can be expressed as love. You can also use this same energy to have a mystical or spiritual experience. When this creative force moves freely, it's what artists and musicians will refer to as "being in the flow." When this energy is repressed, it can then live in the shadow, as discussed on Day 18.

One of my teachers also described this chakra as the womb, because it is a center of potential. This is where our manifestations are born through our desires. The sacral chakra can be a very sensitive and triggering area for some people who have experienced sexual trauma. I hope you hold space for yourself and ask for help if you need more guidance here. Consider reaching out to a womb healer if this is an area of pain for you.

3. Solar Plexus Chakra

Sanskrit: Manipūra; *mani* means "jewel" and *pura* means "city"
Location: Navel point
Element: Fire
Traditional Symbology: Lotus with ten yellow petals
Beej Mantra: Ram
Musical Note: E

This energy center is ruled by the element of fire, and it rules our confidence, self-worth, and the fire that activates us. It governs our willpower and is the driving force that empowers us. Like the sun, the Manipura distributes the solar energy within our body to sustain our vitality. If this energy center is deficient, you might not feel motivated. When we practice Pranayam or breathwork, air is drawn from the belly, the navel point. The air then expands through the lungs, travels through the clavicle, and, finally, is exhaled out of the mouth or nose. In some more intense breathwork practices, you intentionally pump the navel point to create heat and energy. This ignites the fire within. When you fan those flames with your breath (air), it distributes renewed energy all over your body.

4. Heart Chakra

Sanskrit: Anāhata; means "unstruck" or "unbeaten"
Location: The energetic space behind the center of the chest
Element: Air
Traditional Symbology: Lotus with twelve green petals
Beej Mantra: Yam
Musical Note: F

The heart is the most expansive energy center of the body. This is where *shiva*, meaning "consciousness," meets *shakti*, or "creativity." This chakra is the epitome of the saying "listen with your heart." Love, the most heart-centered emotion, is the highest vibration that we as humans can attune ourselves to. It might sound clichéd, but love really is the only force in the world that is real.

The Western world tends to be focused on logic and intellect. People have understood that knowledge and understanding is acquired through the brain, and so we tend to celebrate scholars, great innovators, and analytical thinkers, but we don't necessarily give accolades to people who are heart based. I remember when I was studying in India, my teachers would always ask me, "How are you feeling?" They encouraged me to value my emotional state and to nurture it. When you work with the heart chakra, ask yourself how you are feeling. *The heart is a portal and it's time for us to open up and tune in to what it has to say.* The HeartMath Institute in California studies heart intelligence. On their website they state: "Heart intelligence is the flow of awareness, understanding and intuition we experience when the mind and emotions are brought into coherent alignment with the heart." Try to cultivate heart intelligence—it will serve you particularly well if you feel that this chakra is deficient.

5. Throat Chakra

Sanskrit: Vishuddha; means "purification center"
Location: Throat
Element: Ether
Traditional Symbology: Lotus with sixteen blue petals
Beej Mantra: Ham
Musical Note: G

Communication is your ability to state your needs, share your voice, and articulate your boundaries. The throat is connected to your authenticity. Some people might think that the throat is primarily about speaking, but that's just one aspect of communication. There's also listening. The throat chakra is a broadcasting and receiving station. That means you receive information by listening and you give clarity to your feelings and thoughts through your ability to speak. A lot of the wisdom that we can gain is through stillness and active listening. As I've mentioned, we have nadis, energy channels that are similar to meridians in Traditional Chinese Medicine. There are meridians in our throat that run through our stomach, navel point, and gut area, as well as our solar plexus. These two energy currents have a symbiotic relationship. When you have the confidence to know your worth, it makes sense on an intellectual level. It makes it completely logical to communicate your needs. Work with the throat chakra and you will ask for the raise and promotion automatically when you know you deserve it.

6. Third Eye Chakra

Sanskrit: Ājñā; means "command or monitoring center"
Location: Between the eyebrows
Element: Light
Traditional Symbology: Lotus with two indigo petals
Beej Mantra: Om, pronounced "aum"
Musical Note: A

Unless you have a spiritual understanding, the third eye is going to be elusive. It's going to sound mystical, metaphysical, and new age. This is the command center where we perceive, but in this case it's perception beyond just the physical realm. It's our center of intuition, and the eyes that look inward. When you focus your attention on your third eye, you connect to your higher self, the infinite energy part of you that has lived throughout different lifetimes.

We are three-dimensional beings: mind, body, and soul. The point of awakening to a higher consciousness is not to ascend to it and bypass all of our human experiences but to bring a higher level of consciousness to Earth and instill more truth and enlightenment to the current paradigm.

7. Crown Chakra

Sanskrit: Sahasrāra; means "thousand petaled"
Location: Top of the head
Element: Cosmos
Traditional Symbology: Lotus with one thousand white
    and golden petals
Beej Mantra: Silence
Musical Note: B

If the root chakra is our connection to Mother Earth and the physical realm, the crown is our connection to the cosmos. It's where we can connect to a higher state of consciousness and receive psychic insights. In Maslow's hierarchy of needs, this chakra would correspond to self-actualization. In yoga, it's samadhi (religious trance), and in other spiritual philosophies, enlightenment. I'm not sure we get there fully in human form, but I do know that we can get glimpses of this state through psychedelics, breath work, and deep meditation.

Religious figures such as the pope wear a ceremonial headdress like a mitre or a papal tiara that symbolize power and a direct connection to God. There are many cultures around the world where people wrap their heads in turbans, like the Sikh. Sikh men wear turbans as a symbol of fidelity to their faith, among other reasons. In Sikhism, the skull—in particular, the crown of the head—is a very sensitive part of the body. Wearing a turban is a sign of reverence to God, but it also triggers the pressure points in the skull, which regulates the body and mind. If you've ever been to a Kundalini yoga class, most people will be wearing a turban for similar reasons.

Working with the chakras helps you tune in. It can take time to acquaint yourself with your own subtle energies, so be patient as you digest this information and integrate it into your practice. But the understanding that you are energy and that everything you want is energy will make you believe that manifestation *can be easy*. So it may seem like a lot, but it is worth it to understand the chakra system and the other underlying methodologies I am going to share with you in the following days.

I find working with the chakras especially important when I'm actively manifesting. For example, let's say I am manifesting a creative project. It's so useful to be able to tune in to my chakras to check if they're balanced. I might find that I have an energy deficiency at my sacral chakra, which could indicate writer's block, apathy, or stagnancy. Because the sacral chakra is where ideas are born, I can choose to focus my practices on the sacral chakra to balance it and open it up to the flow. Otherwise, I might have started trying to manifest and immediately hit a wall without knowing quite what was happening. Being able to work with chakras gives you more information when you are assessing your own energy flow, which directly impacts how effective your active manifestations will be. So don't give up, and start small: try the meditation below, and try to process information about each chakra one piece at a time so you don't become overwhelmed.

Body-Scanning Meditation

Sit in a cross-legged position on the floor or sit on a chair with your feet firmly planted on the floor. Now, close your eyes. Take a moment to feel grounded and in the present moment. Take a long, slow deep breath in. Hold it for a moment and then slowly exhale. Breathe in a circular rhythm of inhale and exhale. Allow any tension to melt away as you gradually relax more and more deeply with each breath. Continue to breathe slowly and gently. Relax.

Being aware of your entire body, you are going to scan your chakras, starting from your head to your root. You can also scan your arms and legs. You can visualize, scan with your hands, or both. Bring your awareness to the top of your head, the crown chakra, and notice any sensations or feelings. Notice if you feel expanded or contracted. If you feel contraction, breathe into that area. Even if it's subtle, make a mental note of what you feel here. Does the energy feel like it's flowing? Move down to your third eye, the point between your eyebrows. Move at your own pace. Your throat. Does it feel blocked? Also, notice the sensations in your hands. The hands are secondary heart chakras. Move to your chest, your heart space. Do you feel expanded here? Or contracted? Move to your navel point. Notice any sensations here. Do you feel heat? Coldness? Focus on the womb space, below the navel point. Even if you don't have a womb, everyone has the same energies. Do you feel the flow of energy? What does the sacral feel like? Lastly, you can focus on the area around the base of your spine. Do you feel grounded? Rooted down to earth? When you are ready, you can open your eyes.

GO DEEPER

Simple Energy Healing

If you want to send healing energy to the centers that felt contracted or heavy, you can rub your palms together to activate Source energy. You don't have to be attuned to Reiki, but this is a Reiki technique. Set an intention of sending healing energy to a chakra or chakras. Place your hands on the chakra and focus your attention there, and then repeat in your mind your intention. When you are finished, give thanks to the Universe.

DAY 23
Pleasure and Creation

"There is one great truth on this planet: Whoever you are or whatever it is that you do, when you really want something, it's because that desire originated in the soul of the universe. It's your mission on Earth."
—Paulo Coelho, *The Alchemist*

THE FIRST THING I learned during yoga teacher training in India was how to harness sexual energy to create a desired outcome. My teacher didn't call it manifestation. Just as I mentioned yesterday when we discussed the sacral chakra, the same energy that creates life and babies has the potential to create a project, art, and music.

Pleasure and eroticism do not just mean sex. They represent our ability to tap into our deep creative potential. Many people will say "I'm not creative!" but what they mean is that they don't resonate with traditional meanings ascribed to creativity such as skill in painting or creating music. But we are all creators. We create our lives through our vision, will, and action. When you do the things you are passionate about, you allow the energy to flow. When you allow this energy to flow versus holding it in, you don't project those feelings out as lust or need. When you flow, you instead emit magnetism.

There is an entire chapter in *Think and Grow Rich* by Napoleon Hill on transmutation of sexual energy. Sexual energy can be manifested in many different ways. Most people will relate sexual energy to the act of sexual intercourse. But again, that energy can also be used to be in the flow of creative energy. In this chapter, Hill talks about using this energy to manifest money, because these energies are stored in the same place: they're fundamentally the same.

As Swami Satyananda Saraswati wrote in *Kundalini Tantra*, "Kundalini is creative energy; it is the energy of self-expression." This is the energy we all want to tap into to be in the flow. Do you have a burning desire or passion about something or someone? That's great, because you can redirect that energy not from a place of longing but by channeling that energy into something creative. By creative I don't just mean painting or writing a song, although you could do that—in this case, it means that you can focus the immense creative passion into whatever medium you love. Your love can be the engine driving whatever you are manifesting. From Week 1, you clarified your vision and stated an intention. With that intention, you started to move forward toward your manifestation driven by the power of your desires. So if you feel an overwhelming ardor toward your crush, investigate it: that desire is valid and can be channeled.

Spend time today thinking about your own sexual and erotic energy. What turns you on, and how do you express it? Think about how it feels to be completely overtaken by the energy of passion and meditate using the technique below on how you can direct it in a generative way that will benefit your manifestations.

Creatrix Meditation

POSTURE: Sit in an easy pose, which is a crossed-legged position on the floor. Feel your root chakra grounding down to the earth. Sit with a straight spine.

Close your eyes, take a deep inhale through the nose, and exhale out through the mouth. Do this three times to clear out any stagnant air in your body. When you feel centered, bring both of palms together, uniting your yin and yang sides and connecting at your heart space. Take this moment to call in your higher self, spirit guides, or ancestors if you practice with them. Rub your palms together vigorously so you start to feel the heat between your palms. Your hands are extensions of your heart chakra and therefore will help you to connect to a Higher Intelligence. Place your hands on your sacral chakra, your womb space. Even if you don't have a womb, everyone has this sacred space within them. Take this time to tune in to the energy here. I invite you to send love and healing energy here. You can ask in your mind or out loud these contemplative questions:

- ★ What creation wants to be birthed through me?
- ★ Is there a book that needs to be written? A script? A project?
- ★ How can I channel these energies through my vessel?

If you don't hear any answers, that's okay—you might be asked to do nothing at this time. A mantra you can repeat three times with your hands still at your womb space is: *"I am ready to bring my manifestations to life."*

GO DEEPER

Pleasure Time

Carve out some private time to pleasure yourself. You've heard the saying "Your body is a temple." We can experience bliss and joy through our body. The potential for exploration is limitless. Everyone's experience with pleasure is unique to the individual. Depending on how you were raised to view pleasure, this process might seem taboo, and I honor where you are. You can obviously opt out of this Go Deeper exercise. If you don't feel called to touch yourself, you can lie on your bed, close your eyes, and tune in to your five senses and ask yourself: "What would give me pleasure in terms of sight, touch, taste, smell, and hearing? For example: How would I like to be touched? What would bring pleasure to my body? What would I like to see that would incite pleasure within me? What smells bring me pleasure?"

A mantra you can repeat to yourself is: *I'm a magnificent creature who is worthy of pleasure.*

DAY 24
The Universal Laws

"We live as ripples of energy in the vast ocean of energy."
—Deepak Chopra, *The Way of the Wizard:*
Twenty Spiritual Lessons for Creating the Life You Want

MOST PEOPLE KNOW about the Law of Attraction, which states that like attracts like, but there are many more universal laws. In fact, it is just one of the twelve Hermetic Universal Laws. Becoming familiar with the other eleven can help you unlock a more spiritually aligned life.

The twelve Universal Laws are thought to be intrinsic, unchanging laws of our Universe that ancient cultures have always intuitively known. We can understand the Universal Laws through Einstein's theory of relativity, which shows us that atomic energy vibrates at different rates. His equation $E = mc^2$ proved that energy and matter are the same, and that everything in the universe vibrates at different frequencies.

The same energy that exists all over the universe exists within us. Energy, therefore, is at the basis of all physical reality. From Day 5, we explored that we live in a unified field where all possibilities, realities, and timelines exist. Knowing this, you can shift your reality to the one you want to experience by harnessing your own energy, focusing your thoughts, and working with the Universal Laws. You will recognize many of the same ideas and themes from these laws throughout this book. That's because I employ the twelve Universal Laws throughout my manifestation process, but I did want to present them here for you in an organized way.

When we are born, we each acquire our own unique frequency. Each atom that makes up our physical bodies is vibrating at a specific frequency. For us to manifest, we have to vibrate at the same frequency of our desires. To help you understand this at another level, Dr. Fritz-Albert Popp, who is the founder of the biophoton theory. He has conducted research that confirms the existence of biophotons in our cells. These are particles of light that communicate information within and between cells. He suggests that a human is "essentially, a being of light." We have the ability to change our state of being through our vibration, because different vibrations are difficult to perceive with our human senses. This is why it's necessary to attune ourselves with our "other" senses.

It's only by using our "extra" senses that we can attune to higher perceptions of consciousness, such as our intuition. When we remember that we are made up of the same energy as everything in the universe, it gives us the power to attract infinite possibilities into our lives. The Law of Attraction is about matching energetic frequencies to attract the things we desire into our experience. It is based on the idea that like attracts like—but you can also repel. Whatever you are focused on grows, whether it is good or bad, negative or positive.

You might be asking yourself, "Then why don't I have the thing?" or maybe you are wondering, "Then where is my person?" But maybe "like attracts like" isn't enough. Today, take some time to explore the other eleven Universal Laws and think about ways that you could incorporate them into your daily life to amplify and clarify your visions.

1. The Law of Divine Oneness

The Law of Divine Oneness is the foundational law according to which absolutely everything in our universe is interconnected. In other words, every choice, word, desire, and belief you have will also have an impact on the world and on the people in your life. This Oneness or Source from which everything emanates is an eternal and unchanging unified field of intelligence underlying everything and permeating the whole of creation. Some call it Love, God, the Divine, the Universe, Life Force Energy, or Universal Consciousness.

Yogis, philosophers, astrologers, healers, poets, and artists have channeled through them the idea of oneness. In science, we learned the big bang theory, that this universe started from one big explosion that created everything. As Carl Sagan said, "We are made of star stuff."

Yoga means "union" or "connection." In Sanskrit, the word *yoga* is used to signify any form of connection. Yoga is both a state of connection and a body of techniques that allow us to connect to anything and everything. My favorite Sufi poet, Rumi, expressed this idea through this quote: "You are not a drop in the ocean. You are the entire ocean in a drop." The Law of Divine Oneness is known as the concept of Tao.

2. The Law of Vibration

The principle of vibration is also one of the Hermetic laws of nature: nothing rests, everything moves, everything vibrates. The Law of Vibration states that anything that exists in our universe, whether seen or unseen, can be broken down into and analyzed in its purest and most basic form, which consists of pure energy or light. This material resonates and exists as a vibratory frequency or pattern. All matter, thoughts, and feelings have their own vibrational frequencies.

Everything is energy. Your thoughts, beliefs, and emotions create your vibration. When you change your vibration, everything changes.

Something that really helps me understand this phenomenon is the tuning fork. I'll describe it to you, but please, go on YouTube and watch a video. Two tuning forks are calibrated to the same frequency. If you strike one of them, it begins to vibrate at a specific resonance. The second fork will vibrate, even as it remains untouched. The vibration from the struck tuning fork is transferred to the untouched tuning fork because they are tuned to the same frequency. They are in harmony with vibrations even without physical contact.

3. The Law of Correspondence

Patterns repeat throughout the universe, and these patterns can also be found repeating on a very small scale. For example, think of the popular example of the spiral pattern that reappears in a huge number of places in the galaxy, the Fibonacci sequence. This applies in a figurative sense, too. Look for patterns in your own life and in your thoughts and notice how they repeat elsewhere in the world. As you do so, consider the kinds of pattern changes you might be able to make, and how those will create changes on a larger scale.

In other words, your outer world is a reflection of your inner world. Energy moves in a spiral motion like the galaxy, a DNA helix, the spirals in a caduceus symbol (two snakes winding around a winged staff), tornadoes, a nautilus shell, fingerprints. Everything corresponds to one another on an energetic level.

4. The Law of Attraction

As we've already discussed, the Law of Attraction tells us that like attracts like. To have the things you desire in life, you have to work out how to vibrate on the same frequency as these things. The more general lesson here is that being positive, proactive, and loving attracts more of the same into your life. Meanwhile, pessimism, fear, and lethargy will lead you to generate more negative experiences in all aspects of life. Obviously, there is more nuance to the Law of Attraction, and we cannot always feel positive, so take this as a general overview. Most of the Law of Attraction books I've read try to help you to get into alignment with your desire by being in the same energy. The steps that I've taken away from my studies are as follows:

* Desire—You have a desire to manifest something, so you have to get into a "like" energy to match your desires.
* Imagination—Use your imagination and visualization skills to try to imagine like it's already happening. We explored this during Week 1.
* Affirmation—Say affirmations to help you to reprogram your subconscious mind through repetition. We will do this on Day 26.
* Focus—Focus all your attention on your desire, like we explored on Day 3 when you set an intention.
* Belief—You have to believe that your manifestations are possible, which is what we explored during Week 3 while we were healing our beliefs.
* Gratitude—Give thanks in advance of receiving your manifestation.

Mirror neurons occur when we observe someone doing something and our brains mirror them so that we feel like we are doing the same thing. If we surround ourselves with successful people and positivity, our brains will mirror them, cultivating positive habits and success in our own lives. The Law of Attraction encourages us to surround ourselves with people and circumstances that will bring us closer to our visions.

5. The Law of Inspired Action

The Law of Action must be employed for us to manifest things on Earth. We must engage in actions that support our thoughts, dreams, emotions, and words. The Law of Inspired Action states that you must do the things and perform the actions necessary to achieve what you are setting out to do.

The Law of Attraction requires you to act when you are inspired to create what you want. To get a reaction, you need an action. So it won't just happen: you have to take opportunities if they're presented to you.

You can't just envision, feel, and act *as if* and then expect something to magically fall into your lap. You need to pay attention to the intuitive hunches you get after you do your Law of Attraction rituals, and then follow through by acting on them. There is a difference between knowing and being. The bridge between the two is action.

6. The Law of Perpetual Transmutation of Energy

We all have the power within us to change the conditions of our lives. Higher vibrations consume and transform lower ones. In other words, each of us can change the energies in our lives by understanding the Universal Laws and applying the principles in such a way as to effect change.

For example, if you are feeling grief, you can channel those emotions artistically to create a painting, song, or poem. You've transmuted the pain of grief into a creative expression. This is the principle underlying art therapy. In the same way, if you're angry, you could do some embodiment practices so that the emotion moves through your body and you process it more effectively. Emotions are energy in motion, and they need a way to be expressed through you. Find your favorite ways to create an outlet for your energy to move through you.

7. The Law of Cause and Effect

The Universal Law of Cause and Effect essentially means that every single action will have an equal and opposite reaction. Often, this is thought of as the concept of karma: if you do good, good will come, but if you do bad—watch out. This suggests that the universe is in constant motion and continually progressing. This also means that nothing in life simply "just happens"; it means that everything happens for a reason, even though that reason can be really difficult to see or understand, especially during some of our most challenging times.

This is similar to Newton's third law of motion, which states that for every action there is an equal and opposite reaction. Ralph Waldo Emerson called this the Law of Laws. It's powerful: you get back what you put out. It posits that your actions and thoughts are like a boomerang. You throw them out and they come back.

The principle of cause and effect frees us from the burden of the past and the endless cycle of action and reaction. That means the important thing is not to focus our consciousness on what has already taken place— not to spend our days worrying about and dreading the effects of our past actions. When we dwell on the negative experiences of the past, we continue to attract more and more negative situations.

8. The Law of Compensation

According to the Law of Compensation, you will receive what you put out. This is similar to the Law of Attraction and the Law of Cause and Effect, but with a focus on the idea that compensation can come in many forms. Whatever we do, think, or feel will create a level of compensation equal to the deed we perform. We receive exactly what we deserve for the things we do in our lives, big or small.

The Law of Compensation is important because you get what you give, in return for your efforts, contributions, love, joy, hate, and resentment.

Whatever you give, you get. You will also be compensated—whether that compensation is positive or negative is up to you. You reap what you sow. If you want love, give more love. If you want happiness, spread more happiness. If you want wealth, be generous with wealth. It's that simple. Think about what you're manifesting and give first what you want to receive.

9. The Law of Relativity

The Law of Relativity is all about the neutrality of things when seen in isolation. So no particular person, experience, emotion, or action can be evaluated as good or bad until you look at it in comparison with something else. By keeping this law in mind, you remain conscious of the fact that there are always multiple perspectives on anything that happens to you. Everything is neutral without comparison, and so, ultimately, we can determine the effect an experience will have on us. Trying to slip into these alternate perspectives can make you more grateful and can also show you where you can make improvements in life.

Put simply in the words of Dr. Wayne Dyer, "If you change the way you look at things, the things you look at change." If someone says something negative about us, we have the choice to activate it into our minds. We can either accept it as our reality or reject it.

To practice this law, remember that your entire experience of the world is colored by your beliefs. Everyone acts according to their own experiences and beliefs, which means that you cannot judge another's action because you can never have a full understanding of their history and motivations.

10. The Law of Polarity

When thinking about the Law of Polarity, the most important thing to remember is that absolutely everything has an opposite and that it is the very existence of these opposites that allows us to understand our lives. There is a duality to everything. It's what allows us to experience life to the fullest and appreciate the good in the world even though at times it can be challenging.

Fears and dreams, love and hate, light and dark, north and south, feminine and masculine, yin and yang. The Law of Polarity gives us a powerful tool to change our mindsets: when we understand there is a positive to every negative, we can choose to focus on the positive. The Law of Polarity exists to make you understand that every problem, regardless of its complexity, has a solution within itself, if only you wish to experience it. The key is to balance your experience with duality because integrating the opposing energies creates wholeness.

11. The Law of Rhythm

The Law of Rhythm speaks to movement and how all things in the universe come in cycles. This law might remind you of Day 12, when we "rewilded" ourselves by getting back in touch with our natural cycles. You can see this law abundantly in nature—for example in the seasons and in the body's aging process. However, it applies in the same way to a person's life stages, and reflecting on this helps you to gain perspective. Today's season may be good, but nothing is permanent, so enjoy what you have while it lasts. Alternatively, perhaps you're in a low part of the cycle right now and are suffering, but experiencing pain now may be the very thing that prepares you for a prosperous change in cycles next month.

Everything in existence is a participant in a dance . . . swaying, flowing, swinging back and forth. Life is a spiral. You might be going through a season of your life when your shadows, negative thoughts, or past traumas return. But that may be because the Universe is giving you another chance to heal even more thoroughly now that you have more knowledge and a different perspective.

12. The Law of Sexual Energies

Finally, the Law of Sexual Energies has very little to do with biological sex. Rather, it refers to the fact that there are two major types of energies, the masculine and the feminine. Also known as the yin and yang, being and active, or as anima and animus. We all have both energies regardless of gender and must find a way to achieve a balance between both types if we are to live authentically and happily. Think about the role each type of energy appears to play in your life, and whether there is an excess or a deficiency of either.

Keywords that characterize the Divine Feminine are space, darkness, chaos, softness, passivity, potential energy, age, infinity, and your subconscious mind. The Divine Feminine is like the womb from which all things are created and can never be destroyed. Like energy, it is the foundation of all creation. The Divine Feminine is the "is-ness" or the "being" of all things.

The Divine Masculine's keywords are specificity, light, structure, hard, order, kinetic energy, creativity, activity, youth, the new, and your conscious mind. The Divine Masculine is the point of focus in this now-moment that pulls the energy "is-ness" into form and brings it into manifest creation. The Divine Masculine is the action or the "doing."

Though it isn't necessarily the thirteenth law, The Law of Resonance is what you attract based on an emotional response. It is worth considering during this journey, as it has relevance to manifestation. The Law of Resonance states that the rate of vibration projected will harmonize with and attract back energies with the same resonance. This determines whether you are in fear or love.

Notice what is resonating with you at this current time. Look at what you're attracting and see if it's something that you want to experience or not. Try not to judge yourself here—energy can shift in an instant once you bring awareness to it. For example, if you only have friends around you who put you down and don't support you, you are not resonating on the frequency of love. If you want to attract supportive friends, this is an opportunity for you to ask yourself, "Why am I resonating below the frequency of love?" Maybe there's something internally that you have to pay attention to? Keep asking yourself, "How can I resonate more on the frequency of love?" You can always tune in to your Higher Power for guidance.

Approaching the Universal Laws

In your journal, write down all twelve of the Universal Laws and the Law of Resonance. Meditate and see how each of these play out in your life. Can you give examples from your own observations of each? Maybe you'll realize you need to work on one specifically and you'll want to do a deep dive. For example, if you realize you want to understand the Law of Rhythm and be more in sync with nature, you could start studying sacred geometry with a specialist. That's what I did, and it was so fascinating and useful. She had me look at repeating patterns in nature and how I observed these patterns in my own life. I started to sync up my life to the cycles of the moon and the astrological seasons. Based on these energies, I inherently knew when to rest and when to take action. I also started eating foods in season and from local farmers. Just understanding this one Universal Law and how everything is connected had a huge ripple effect on my whole life for the better.

GO DEEPER

Focus on one of the Universal Laws that you want to focus on and research, investigate, and start getting to work on it.

DAY 25
Scripting

"Ask for what you want and be prepared to get it."
—Maya Angelou

SCRIPTING IS A Law of Attraction technique where you write a new story about your life based on how you want it to be. Scripting requires you to write your story as if it has already happened or is happening right now by focusing on how you would feel when your desires are manifested.

We create stories about ourselves that might not reflect our reality. We've explored how your way of seeing yourself and the world is biased based on your experience, how you were raised, where you grew up, and whatever other factors shaped your worldview. This perspective gets even more distorted based on what you consume: stories in media such as movies and TV, highlighted posts on social media, aspirational visions from advertising. We so often create narratives in our heads about why we can't do something. But the good news about that tendency is that we can rewrite those narratives.

Our stories elicit emotions that motivate our behavior. Scripting helps us to write our own story, and while we write it, the process helps us to feel as if it's happening now. This is in no way spiritually bypassing the work of actually experiencing these events, because during the rest of this journey, we will be continuing to do the work from the previous weeks. You can't create a new story until you know the root cause of your old one. But scripting can help us create a vision of what the future could be, even as we are working with the origins of our trauma. I believe that we are multidimensional beings, which means that we can simultaneously heal our past and create a new future. In fact, we must dream, because if we are only healing the past, we will get burned out and forget why we are healing in the first place.

There's a reason why most manifestation teachers tell you to write down what you are manifesting. At the beginning of every year, I write down five things that I want to manifest. And while I don't always manifest everything on the list, it helps me to focus on my goals and what I'm calling in.

I do want to suggest that if you're new to scripting, writing down your manifestations, or manifesting in general, you might want to start small. Meaning you'll want to start from a place where you can believe in what you're writing down. If you currently have zero dollars in your bank account and you write that you're a millionaire, your mind is not going to believe it—you're going to build resistance. Start with statements that you can believe more intuitively, like "I am receiving money every day." Your mind will be more open and receptive to manifesting $100 versus $100,000. Once you manifest $100, increase it to $500, and so on. Once you build momentum, your mind will believe in the process more, and it will get easier.

When you read your new story, try to feel as if you're the main character. It's like Atreyu in *The Neverending Story*: the more he reads the story, the more he gradually becomes the main character. You are upgrading your current operating system by the power of auto-suggestion. The subconscious mind is malleable, and you can create new neural pathways. Please don't get discouraged if this takes time, because it took time to get you here and it will take the same amount of time to unwind some of your accumulated beliefs.

In his Netflix documentary *Shawn Mendes: In Wonder*, singer and songwriter Shawn Mendes reveals his manifestation journaling. In one scene, he shares his mantras and scripting process by writing sentences over and over again (in other words, auto-suggestion through repetition). He shows one page out of the journal where he wrote, "I will sell out the Rogers Centre." This was days before he was slated to perform at that venue. And in the end, he did exactly what he scripted—he manifested it.

Write down your life as if it's a powerful spell. You are conjuring it. Powered with your vision and your belief, watch as the magic unfolds. When we want something and we are waiting for it to show up, it can create an energy of attachment. Instead of saying, "Where is this person? Where is my manifestation?" rephrase your statements to "I am open to love. I am receiving love. I am deserving of love. I have so much love to give."

Asian Canadian actor Simu Liu has been tweeting Marvel Studios since 2014 about bringing an Asian superhero to the screen. Not only did he pitch himself, he also posted shirtless photos of himself exemplifying his readiness for the job. In 2018, when there were talks of casting *Shang-Chi and the Legend of the Ten Rings*, Simu wrote directly to Marvel and asked, "Are we gonna talk or what?" It seems to me that Simu Liu tweeted to Marvel and the Universe very clearly what he wanted.

In his 1949 book, *The Hero with a Thousand Faces*, author Joseph Campbell wrote extensively about what he called the hero's journey. The hero's journey has three main parts: departure, initiation, and return. You will recognize this story structure in most books and films. It's also a useful structure to use as you script your story. Each of us has a positive and a negative story that both guide how we move through life. This is an opportunity for you to write a new, more positive story.

Crafting Your Hero's Journey

Write your new story in the present tense. Here are some questions to help you:

★ What time do you get up in the morning? Are you woken up by an alarm?

★ Do you have a partner? Family? Pets?

★ Where do you live?

★ What does your home look like?

★ You are getting ready for the day. What kind of clothes are you wearing?

★ Do you work from home?

★ How do you spend your day?

★ What do you do for fun and pleasure?

★ What kinds of adventures do you go on?

★ What do you create?

GO DEEPER

Read your story every morning and night to feed auto-suggestions to your subconscious mind.

DAY 26
Affirmations

"I believe you can speak things into existence."
—Jay-Z

I WENT THROUGH a period of life during which I integrated a lot of what I've learned from Christianity, Buddhism, Hinduism, and other different spiritual philosophies I was exploring. One of the things I was most curious about was why the *Word* was the first thing that happened in the beginning of all creation, according to the Bible.

My belief, both then and now, is that God brought the Universe into being by speaking it out loud. As I mentioned previously, everything has a frequency, a vibration, and a resonance, because everything is energy. You emit a specific frequency. When you speak, your voice has a specific vibration. When you speak, you are sending out signals to the Universe—I mentioned tuning forks resonating with each other earlier in this journey. When you speak words, something on the other side vibrates to match it and becomes attracted to you by the Law of Attraction.

When spoken aloud, your words are spells. When you speak out to the Universe, you are performing an incantation. Similar to scripting and writing, you are *spelling*. As I mentioned on Day 1, you are manifesting all the time. You are manifesting right now. And if you want to manifest something different, watch what you say.

Louise Hay was a master of so many techniques, but she had particularly resonant things to say about affirmations. As she said, "An affirmation opens the door." She believed that spoken words are the beginning of change. In essence, affirmations are the way you communicate with your subconscious mind, taking responsibility for change and acknowledging your responsibility in what will happen. She wrote about the importance of consciously choosing the right words to manifest what you desire, "words that will either help eliminate something from your life or help create something new in your life." Words have the power to change both your internal and external worlds.

In an interview with Anderson Cooper on *60 Minutes*, Lady Gaga shared that her favorite manifestation technique was repeating affirmations. She would repeat to herself that she was famous even when she wasn't. She said, "You repeat it to yourself every day. And it's not yet, it's a lie. You're saying a lie over and over again, and then, one day the lie is true." As you know, the rest is history, because she became the star she is today.

When I first learned about Dr. Masaru Emoto's water experiments, it changed the way I saw everything—but more important, how I spoke to myself. Dr. Masaru Emoto was a Japanese businessman and author of the *New York Times* bestselling book *The Hidden Messages in Water*. In his experiments, he labeled various water glasses and then exposed them to different kinds of music, affirmations, pictures, and words. The changes he observed were remarkable. He used microscopic photography to capture the water's molecular structure and found that it had reordered itself corresponding to the material to which it had been exposed.

To a glass of water that was labeled *love*, he said, "I love you." By contrast, he said, "You're ugly" to the water labeled *ugly*. The one that received love looked like a perfect snowflake. The "ugly" one had no form and looked distorted. Dr. Emoto even found that when polluted water was given a healing intention and prayer, the structure of the water also changed and was no longer polluted.

This gives new meaning to thoughts and prayers. Our human bodies are made of 75 percent water. So why would you say unkind words to yourself, or expose yourself to negative emotions? If the simple words "I love you" could reorder the molecular structure of a glass of water and compel it to assume the shape of a perfect snowflake—a generative and beautiful shape found in nature—imagine what saying "I love you" to yourself, or exposing yourself to the energy of love, could do.

Water is a wonderful medium for purification, healing, and manifestation. Exposing yourself to this mutable, receptive element can bring you back into balance. If you have access to an ocean, take a dip and ask the ocean to cleanse you. If you have a bath, fill it with Epsom salt and speak your intentions aloud. If you think about it, we began our life in the watery womb of our mother. Water is where creation began. Water is a powerful medium for manifestation.

Just to reiterate the Law of Divine Oneness, and the Hermetic principle of as within, so without, as above, so below. Seventy-five percent of Earth's surface is covered with water. The moon has a magnetic pull on Earth. Scientists have proven that the full moon, in particular, raises the tides of the oceans around the world. When the tides of the oceans rise on Earth, the emotional body within humans also rises. This is why energy healers and astrologers believe that full moons come with heightened emotional states. Lastly, the moon's phases are twenty-eight days, and so is a female's moon cycle or menstruation cycle.

If you look at this world with the feeling of scarcity—that nothing works out for you—and you feel it and believe it, that is exactly what you will receive. Once, I was talking to one of my cousins and, exasperated by what he perceived as my lack of pragmatism, he said, "I live in reality, and not everyone can follow their dreams." To that, I said, "That's very true for your reality, because you're saying it to me and you believe that." Again, words are spells. They are powerful. So while they can create amazing things, also be very careful and mindful of what you say, because you could be unintentionally creating a reality you don't want.

Be mindful of how you say things like "I need to make money" because "make" implies that you will literally create money, when in reality, you're not saying you need to chop down a tree, make the wood into paper, and then print cash. And similarly, when you say that you "need" something, it implies that you don't have it. Some of you might need money to pay your rent, and your survival depends on it, and I'm not telling you to deny what you are going through. Just be careful of how you use your words to describe your situation. You can try to say, "I'm open to figuring out my situation. I'm healing my money story, I'm creating more value within myself and therefore, in exchange, I receive money for it." Like I said in Week 2, when we discussed alignment, you receive money automatically by providing value. The more value you give, the more money you receive.

Affirmations

If you use a smartphone, in your voice notes app or any other recording apps, record "I am" affirmations for at least five minutes and listen every day during your walk or meditation. Some examples are: "I am open to receiving, I am open to love, I am walking toward my abundance. I am healthy, I am beautiful, I am pure love and energy."

GO DEEPER

Create a Moon Water Ritual

Before I get into the ritual, I want to introduce you to the phases of the moon that can provide the best energy to work with. Plan to do this on the new or full moon. Please take into consideration a void of course moon. A void of course moon is the time when the moon makes its last aspect to when the moon changes signs. It's said to be a time when the moon rests and rejuvenates, so energetically, it's not a good time to start anything new. A void of course moon is not a good time to set intentions or do a ritual—nothing will come from it. You can do an Internet search for when the void of course moon is in connection to the moon phase during which you are doing your ritual.

Get a glass jar or mason jar that has a top. Fill up your glass jar with water. Set up your ritual space (for suggestions see page 33). If you've kept your altar from Day 4 maintained, that is an excellent place to do this ritual. Clear the area energetically, or with local herbs or incense. Light a candle and create some space for yourself to meditate on your intention. Your intention can be healing, vitality, more energy, more hope, more love. Hold your glass jar of water between your hands. Take a deep inhale from the belly. Pause for a few seconds. Then exhale all the air out of your mouth. State your intention out loud. Feel the energy coming out of you through your hands. You can say a prayer to your water. At that point, you can either drink all of it in one sitting, or you can drink a sip each day for a week. If you have enough water, you can do this for fourteen days, taking a sip each day through the next two moon phases. As you drink the water, remember Dr. Emoto's water studies and the power of your intentions.

DAY 27
Emotions: Energy in Motion

"Whatever you wish to manifest, associate a feeling
of love with it and impress that feeling on the universal
subconscious mind—and it will do the rest."
—Dr. Wayne Dyer, *Wishes Fulfilled*

WE MANIFEST FROM our feelings, our state of being. Today is all about separating thoughts from feelings and getting your emotional state into alignment with your vision.

To manifest, you must align your thoughts, beliefs, and feelings to your desire. You can say affirmations all day long. You can create one hundred vision boards, take ritual baths, or meditate for hours. But if you don't *feel* it, you're going to have issues. This is where the phrase "act *as if*" comes in, and it used to frustrate the hell out of me. Nobody in my family has ever written a book or has been visible on social media. Growing up, I had Connie Chung to look up to, but other than her, there were not many Asian American women represented in the media at that time. As a result, believing success in any kind of media was possible for me seemed pretty far-fetched.

While I've been writing this book, I've been thinking about all the times when I manifested something successfully. I spent a lot of time remembering what that sensation felt like. What I eventually realized was that I can't articulate the feeling of a successful manifestation for you, because you will have to cultivate it for yourself. Everyone has a unique experience, and the emotions that make it happen are all you. All I can say is that there's a deep knowing. You will know it, even though you don't see it.

This is also where your wild imagination will come in handy. As a kid, I would spend hours daydreaming and conjuring up visions in my mind. I used to get into trouble for drifting off and gazing out the window, but now I realize it's my superpower. Use your imagination to access the feelings that will bring you closer to your manifestation. I have to say that, for my part, when I got this book deal, I was super excited—but I wasn't entirely surprised, because I had already lived it in my mind. In there, it had already happened.

You can't necessarily change the way you feel, but you can filter your thoughts. You can reprogram your mind to elicit a feeling and emotion. Humans act on their feelings. When the feeling is powerful enough, you are mobilized to act, because action is necessary to create the life of your dreams and manifest. Thoughts alone are just concepts.

Our emotions are usually triggered by an external stimulus. For example, your mom says something that triggers you, and then you get angry and yell at her. Your mom's words are the stimulus, and anger is the emotion they produce. And remember, all emotions are valid and useful, even if they're negative, because they contain information. Emotions are energy in motion—they are meant to move through us and be experienced. However, we are not meant to cling to these emotions. We need outlets through which we can channel our emotions. Some of my favorite ways to do this are through energy healing like Reiki, exercising, dancing, and breath work. And if things get really overwhelming, don't rule out screaming! Anything to feel what you need to feel and get where you need to be.

In both psychology and energy healing, we talk about emotional regulation. Emotional regulation happens when we choose to leave an emotional state—let's say, sadness or apathy. Keep in mind I am not talking about mental illness. If you are dealing with something overwhelming that can't be exorcised with the techniques I've mentioned, please seek a licensed professional and talk to a therapist. However, in terms of temporary states, it's necessary to emotionally regulate by reviewing your thoughts. What kinds of things are you consuming? What kind of food are you eating? What kinds of social media are you scrolling through? Who are you surrounding yourself with? All of these sources of stimuli might be impacting your mental health and how you're feeling. Do an inventory.

We can change our thoughts more easily than we can change our emotions and behaviors. When we can change our thoughts, it ignites a "feeling" response, and that will either motivate us or disempower us. Choose your thoughts wisely. This is where curiosity is key, and why I love Gemini, the most mercurial, flighty, and super-chatty sign in the zodiac. Geminis are possessed with unending confidence and curiosity about the world around them, and they don't stop to criticize themselves. So when you have a negative belief about yourself, like, "I'm not smart enough to start my own business," ask yourself, "Where's the proof? Could I be wrong? There are plenty of billionaires out there who are not college graduates," or so on. Redefine what success means for you individually. Not everyone strives to be a narcissistic egomaniac worth billions of dollars shooting out into space—so you definitely don't have to either!

We have to feel so fully that it radiates out of our cells, our energy, our auras, out of our being. The feeling has to override the doubts in your mind, because doubts will always be there. Having doubts is just a part of being human.

When I was in my twenties, my boyfriend at the time shared with me that when we first got together, when we were just friends, he spent every lunch break for an entire summer daydreaming about me, picturing us together, and he said it made him feel happy. I remember the summer he spoke of, because I was feeling the same way. It took us many years to go from friends to lovers, but it was an experience that we definitely manifested. It confirmed to me that *what you seek is seeking you too,* and if it's aligned, it cannot miss you. The relationship didn't last because I believe certain people come into our lives, we learn something from each other, and they are meant to leave. I don't have scientific proof, and this is just anecdotal life experience of mine. I've learned that when we love someone, one of the best things we can do for them is to let them go.

You can also notice when you get jealous of someone. Notice what they have that triggers you. That feeling is your heart saying, "I want this too! But why can't I have it?" The answer is: you can! Take your gaze off the other person and start to reflect that energy back toward yourself and ask yourself, "What do I need to do to get that?"

An indicator of how you will know that your manifestations are on the way is if you feel it with every cell of your being. Because your body is already there and you're already living it. As Neville Goddard states in his book *Feeling Is the Secret*, "Sensation precedes manifestation and is the foundation upon which all manifestation rests." Work on how you feel and what you want to experience from your manifestations then ask the Universe for this or something better.

Thoughts versus Feelings

Try to understand your thoughts versus your feelings. Here is a technique that will help you sort out the two.

1. Observe your thought. What is the content of your thought?
2. Is it true? Answer without judgment.
3. What is the evidence of its validity?
4. Move the thought out of your head and into your body. When the thought is just in our head, it prevents us from understanding our own feelings. To embody this thought, put on your favorite song to dance to and move your body. Nobody is watching you, so go wild. Whip your hair, jump up and down, sweat it out.

5. Notice how you feel afterward. Did anything come up
   during your dance session?
6. Did any emotions surface? Are your feelings in
   alignment with your thoughts?
7. Do you feel better or worse?

GO DEEPER

Try an ecstatic dance class

Ecstatic dance is a type of dance that allows you to feel
the music in your body and express yourself by freestyle
movement. There are no particular choreographed dance
moves, so it's more of an opportunity for self-expression
through your body. The ecstatic dance classes I've been to
have been varied. Some of them have an intention of moving out negative emotions. Others felt like a community
dance party. It's a really great way to have fun, move your
body, heal, laugh, and get some of that stagnant energy
out. If there are no ecstatic dance classes in person near
you, you can always search online and on YouTube, then
dance along to any videos you find.

DAY 28
Shifting Your Reality

"It matters not what someone is born but what they grow to be."
—Albus Dumbledore, *Harry Potter and the Goblet of Fire*

BECAUSE OUR MANIFESTATIONS come from our state of mind, the quickest way to manifest is to *feel* as if what we desire is happening right now. On Day 11, we talked about the importance of being in the present moment. You can only manifest from the present moment, because *now* is the only time that's real. Eckhart Tolle's *The Power of Now* says it all in the title. The book is about how living in the now will give you inner peace. According to Tolle, this liberates your mind from the illusions of the ego. Living in the now is a concept we'll take into our practice today.

The aspect of yourself that is a multidimensional spirit understands that time is not real. There's only now. But, because your ego aspect needs time to help you function in your human existence, you don't experience time on that spiritual level. We need "clock time" to organize our lives—to schedule meetings and appointments, to wake up and go to sleep and eat meals. But, because your brain divides time in this way, it has a tendency to look in either direction, particularly when you are experiencing difficulties. And this tends to compound your problems: if you are dwelling in the past, your body and your mind are living in the past. If you are waiting for outside circumstances to change how you feel, you are living in the future. In either case, your temporal displacement will cause more anxiety and stress and keep you from manifesting any reality that you are trying to envision.

My yoga philosophy teacher told us that we have to be the observers of our lives. We have to understand that we are both the egoic personality and divinity and not become too attached to either so that we can live a balanced life. We need our ego because we are human. We need to understand a linear timeline of the past, present, and future—but we don't need to be trapped in the illusion of time. This keeps us feeling like something is lacking or missing in our lives. When we live like this, it's so easy to think, "I'll be so happy when I . . ." get the job, meet the right person, make a million dollars. And what is even more detrimental is when you begin to feel like the now is too painful, so you resist what is—you bypass it, or you live in denial. When we bypass our real, lived experiences, we miss so much: opportunities to learn, exorcise feelings that must be processed, and meet the shadow parts of ourselves before they break into our day-to-day lives and cause us pain.

If you want to experience a "future" you, someone who has already manifested the thing you are calling in, feel it now. Be happy now. Live in joy now. If you can imagine a version of yourself out there who is living your dream life in a parallel reality, tune in to that person's energy and start merging with that timeline. Allow yourself to tap in to who this person is by asking concrete questions like "What do they look like? What are they wearing?"

It's tough: when we manifest, we are intending to bring into our current life that which we do not currently have. And it can be genuinely difficult to feel a thing that you don't see yet. Shifting your reality in this way can absolutely mess with your mind, because you'll want to see it to believe it, but remember: it's about believing first, and *then* you will see it.

My mom's big manifestation was immigrating to the United States. Ever since she was a little girl, she dreamed of moving to the United

States, where it was, she thought, the land of possibilities. She loved the music, movies, the whole culture. I asked my mom how she manifested it, and she said that she would look up at the sky and just know that one day she would live in the United States. There were definitely some action steps she took to try to make that happen. She was thinking about enrolling in culinary school and coming to the United States on a student visa. But what she really wanted me to reiterate in telling her story was that she didn't know how it was going to happen—she just believed it would. My mom was a teacher in South Korea at the time she was introduced to my dad through one of the students at her school. This student would become my aunt. For three months, my parents "dated" through mail. You read that right: they had only known each other through snail mail. My dad was already living in New York at the time. He flew to Korea to meet my mom and get married, and when they got married, she got her ticket to the United States.

The *unified field theory* was initially proposed by Albert Einstein. It is meant to provide an explanation that ties all phenomena together within the universe. According to Einstein, we are all matter and energy, and so we are all related on a molecular level. The unified field theory reminds me of the Law of Divine Oneness, which is a tenet of most spiritual and religious beliefs. In so many different religious and spiritual traditions, we are all connected. We are part of the whole while being individually whole. So when you do something loving to yourself, you do something loving to the whole, and when you do something hurtful to yourself, you hurt the whole. To extend this to our perception of time: past, present, and future are not discrete entities. Our actions have singular meanings that exist in multiple timelines, and the "you" of the present is the only real you there is. You can't turn your back on "past you" or discount what you're doing now while looking to a perfect future. You are you.

All possibilities and realities exist in this timeline. Everything that is real or imagined exists. Shift your focus and energy to it and believe it's possible, then give yourself gratitude for already possessing the thing you desire.

This is how it happens: the fifth dimension is our astral body, our feelings. The astral body is the spiritual etherlike counterpart to our physical bodies. In other words, the astral body is the energy system associated with our emotional experiences. We have a desire for something. We receive intuitive hits from the unified field. We bring those down to the third dimension—the physical realm—through our actions. That is manifestation: when thoughts become things.

So if you say to the unified field, "All the good men are taken" or "Men suck," that is what the field will deliver to you. Your life is a mirror of your perceptions. That is why we set an intention by doing a morning routine or ritual. If you spend the first hour after you wake up and the last hour before you sleep suggesting to your subconscious mind that your person is out there, it helps your mind to believe, and in turn, it helps you achieve.

When you send out your intentions, the Universal Law of Cause and Effect must respond. For every action, there's an equal and opposite reaction. If I say, "It's so hard to make money," the Universe will react and deliver that.

The unified field shows its presence in our lives in so many different ways. Once you begin to think about it, you'll see these connections as well. If you have a dream about someone and the next morning that person texts you, that's the unified field. If you spend time thinking about someone and that person contacts you, it was the unified field responding to what you threw out into the Universe. Take the time to shift your reality so that when you send out your intentions, they are met with the responses you desire.

Contemplate the Current You

Spend time thinking about what you need to think, believe, feel, and do to bridge the gap between the current you and the future you. What does the current you need to release to believe the future you is possible? What does the current you need to learn, read, and experience for you to get there? Write in your journal or meditate on these questions.

GO DEEPER

Shifting Realities Meditation

The Setup

1. Using a voice recording app, record these instructions in your own voice, and then listen to the recording while you meditate. Read the script at a slow pace so you hear and experience each word.
2. Try to take long pauses (five to ten seconds) between each sentence.
3. Sit on the floor in a cross-legged position. If that's difficult, sit in a chair with your spine straight and feet firmly planted on the floor. Take a few deep breaths and calm your body and mind.
4. Close your eyes.

Take a deep inhale through your nose and let go as you breathe out through your mouth. Bring awareness to your breath. Notice every sensation in your body as you breathe in and out. Everything slows down into the present moment. Feel your heart beating and the energy expanding. Feel yourself being fully present in the moment. Acknowledge that you are here now. In this expansive moment. You can hear, smell, and sense. Your physical senses can tell you that you're here now. Your sit bones are rooting down to the chair or the floor. You know you are here. There is more here than your physical senses are aware of. The energy of your dreams and desires is already here in vibrational form. What if your reality is shifting so that you can feel your dreams and desires now? What if you can align your energy to the energy of your dreams and desires by feeling it now? You are closer than you think. Open up and expand your mind, and ask yourself, "What if it is here now?" Feel it with your open and expansive heart.

Imagine in your mind's eye the energy of your heart expanding and picking up on the vibration of your dreams and desires. What does it feel like? You are merging with this energy now. It's already here. Stay with this feeling and allow the visions to come into your mind. What does your environment look like? Who are you with? What are you wearing? What kinds of things are you doing? Live in the moment and bask in the energy now. When you are ready, bring awareness into your physical body and your physical space and open your eyes slowly. Journal anything that comes up for you. Most important, focus on how you feel.

Week 5

DAYS 29–35

Your New State of Being

In Week 5, you'll begin to enter the reality you've begun to create for yourself. Now that you are aligned and in the flow, you'll call in your soul family, begin to cultivate your extrasensory perception, live in abundance, and finally take the action steps you'll need to manifest what you most desire!

DAY 29
Becoming Whole

"The quest for wholeness can never begin on the external level.
It is always an inside job."
—Dr. Shefali Tsabary

HELLO, BEAUTIFUL SOUL! This week is all about the new you: your new identity, which is you vibrating at a higher frequency. This didn't come about because the old you was bad, but because you are getting closer to who you really are. You've been taking the steps to remember who you've always been this whole time. Today, we will talk about *wholeness*, which is essential to our understanding of manifestation. Successful manifestations come from a place of wholeness—health, wealth, abundance, and joy.

In the introduction to this journey, I mentioned the etymology of the word *wealth*. The word *wealth* shares its etymology with *health*, *well-being*, and *wholeness*. Health, wealth, and well-being are part of our natural state, so it's up to us to investigate where the blocks are. Week 3 was all about healing to become well again, not because there was something wrong, but because there was an imbalance—a dis-*ease*. You forgot about who you really are. Maybe you gave your power away. You felt small and you did this because you didn't have the tools when you needed them.

This is where the forgiveness journey came in. We learned to call back those lost parts of yourself and took time to love that "past" you who didn't know any better. You did the best you could with the information and the tools that you had at the time. That's why we brought our shadow parts to the surface, because our light and dark make us whole. I used to hide my chaotic and weird energy from people (except for my family, of course) because I thought people would only like the "perfect" version of me that I projected to be accepted. I had to trust that the people who were worthy of me would love all of me. When you let it all out, you'll know exactly who and what you need, and then you'll be able to make choices that lead to wholeness.

Today is a culmination of all the lessons we have experienced together. What you have learned has led you to this very important place of wholeness. I want you to remember Week 2, when we explored alignment. We all have the same purpose here on Earth, which is to fully know and love ourselves, and to share our stories, which brings in more love.

Humans need to be seen, heard, and accepted in a community. Being accepted impacts us at a psychological, emotional, and spiritual level. When you feel that you are separate, you will not feel safe. If you don't feel safe, it's hard to trust, and if you don't trust, it's hard to be in the flow. Safety, trust, and being in the flow are all imperative in the manifestation process. You must look in the mirror and see yourself, hear yourself, accept yourself, and build your worthiness from within.

You need to know exactly who you are regardless of other people's opinions and expectations. Then, build up your confidence and share your story with others. I can bet there will be people out there who will resonate with your story in some way. Be vulnerable and take down the mask of who you think you need to be and just share your truth. Doing this gives other people the permission to do the same. When you give more value to others, you receive in kind.

It's likely that you want to manifest something because you feel that you aren't currently experiencing it. Conversely, you are experiencing the lack of it. What we default to is looking outside of ourselves to fill that lack. For example, if you're trying to manifest a romantic partner and you manifest from this place of lack—because you feel that you don't already have that kind of love in your life—you will attract that same lack-of-love energy back to you. You will keep attracting your current state of mind unless you look within and heal this feeling of lack. To manifest a romantic partner, first you'll need to experience love and whatever feelings that you believe a romantic partner will give you. Those qualities could be security, safety, companionship, or all of the above. Sometimes, when we look inside ourselves to place names on our desires, we find that they are darker: obsession, addiction, codependency. There's no judgment here—only awareness. Until you address the content of those feelings, you will not attract what it is you are seeking. So be honest with yourself and force yourself to look.

Our relationships help bring us closer to ourselves. That includes all kinds of relationships—not just romantic. The relationships we have with ourselves, our family, our friends, and the other people with whom we interact can focus our own hearts, clarify our needs and desires, and allow us to cultivate conscious awareness around our triggers and subconscious projections. The best we can do for others is to become conscious. When two conscious people come together, they can have a deeply intimate and fulfilling relationship, and they can help each other on their individual journey toward wholeness.

Become whole first. Become *holy*—not in the religious sense, but in the sense that you are on a heroine's journey through the landscapes of your emotions and psyche, and everything you see is sacred. If you are poor, feel rich now; if you are single, feel love now. That's where you'll find the work you need to do to get to the next step.

How do you feel whole without the thing or person you're wishing for? Through joy, and the act of radiating that feeling out and into the world. The more joy you feel, the more whole and complete you'll feel, and that's the energy you will attract. The energy of joy activates our feeling of well-being, and remember, well-being is wholeness. Today's meditation will help you to tune in to the energy and the feeling of what you're manifesting. Just know that if you can conjure the feeling from within you, you already have it.

Meditation for Creating Your Future

This meditation will help you to clear your mind and focus on one word that represents what you want to manifest for the future. Make sure you have a timer to keep track of the time.

POSTURE: Sit in Easy Pose, which is a cross-legged position on the floor. Stretch the spine up and become very still. You can begin your practice by tuning in with the Adi mantra:

1. Close your eyes and bring your palms together in prayer mudra with your thumbs touching your sternum. Focus your attention on your third eye, the point between your eyebrows.
2. Inhale through the nose and exhale out through mouth.
3. Inhale halfway and start to chant *ong namo guru dev namo.* Chant this three times. Try to chant in one breath: *ong namo guru dev namo* is the golden chain. When you chant it, you are bowing down to the teachers before you and the teacher within. *I bow to the subtle divine wisdom, I bow to the divine teacher within.*
4. Feel the vibration that you have created.
5. When you are ready, you can open your eyes.

Part One

EYE FOCUS: Eyes are closed.
POSTURE: Continue to sit in Easy Pose with a straight spine.
MUDRA: Place your hands palms down on the knees.
BREATH WORK: Breath of Fire

1. Focus your attention on your navel point (solar plexus). As you exhale forcefully through your nose,

your inhales will be automatic and passive. As you
exhale, your navel point snaps toward your spine.
Imagine there are embers there and you need breath
to create a fire. The exhale should be in a rhythmic
beat try to do it, one breath per second. If you
start to feel dizzy or light-headed and it makes you
uncomfortable, you can take deeper breaths and do
it slowly. Similarly, if you are pregnant or on the first
three days of your menstrual cycle, please refrain from
this breath work and take slow, deep breaths. Do this
for three minutes.

There are many benefits of Breath of Fire. We are waking up your chakras
and clearing your energy field. Just imagine that every breath lights up the
fire within you, and the energy moves down past your sacral to your root.
Then, your life-force energy rises back up your sushumna nadi (main channel) through the rest of your chakras. It might be difficult to keep this up for
three minutes, but stick with it, because you will feel clear afterward.

Part Two

EYE FOCUS: Eyes are closed. Focus on your third eye, the point
between your eyebrows.

POSTURE: Continue to sit in Easy Pose with a straight spine.

MUDRA: Place your hands in Gyan mudra, with your thumb and index
finger of each hand touching to make a ring shape. The other three fingers
are together, splayed out. Place your Gyan mudras on your knees, palms
up. Mudras are hand gestures that direct energy to or away from us, and
this one specifically calls in the Infinite Intelligence.

BREATH WORK: Inhale through the mouth with pursed lips. Imagine you're sipping all of the abundance, love, and prosperity in the Universe that you are calling in. Hold the breath at the top and, when you do,
bring to your third eye and your awareness in one word what you want

to manifest (for example, love, prosperity, peace, children, joy, pleasure, home). Then exhale out through your nose. When you bring the word to your mind, really feel it in your body. Allow yourself to connect to the energy of it. Keep repeating this for seven minutes.

Close

On the last inhale, raise your arms over your head and spread your fingers, your palms facing out. Hold the breath for seven counts, squeeze your lower chakras, the perineum, sex organs, navel. Allow the energy to expand. Then exhale deeply one last time while bringing down your arms. You can keep your eyes closed and stay here for a few minutes. Chant the Sat Nam mantra three times. The *sat* is long (saaaaaaat), and the *nam* is short (nam). *Sat Nam* means "truth is my identity."

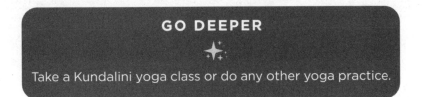

GO DEEPER

Take a Kundalini yoga class or do any other yoga practice.

DAY 30
Intuition

*"Your conscience shouts, 'Here's what you should do,' while
your intuition whispers, 'Here's what you could do.' Listen to
that voice that tells you what you could do."*
—Steven Spielberg, Harvard commencement address, 2016

I'VE BEEN ALLUDING to intuition during this entire journey with you. That's because your intuition is so important in the manifestation process: a well-developed sense of intuition will never steer you in the wrong direction, so it can help you know when your visions will bring you to the reality you desire, whether the Universe is sending you signs, and when to take action based on those signs. Our intuition speaks to us through flashes of insight, moments of déjà vu, goose bumps, a fluttering heart, a tight feeling in the stomach. Unlike our five senses that help us perceive the physical world—touch, see, hear, taste, and smell—intuition is multidimensional. So, even though we all get intuitive hits, we have to learn when to trust them, so we don't default to our logical minds and override them. To be able to perceive the subtle realms, it's necessary to practice: as with muscles, pushing yourself to use your intuition on a regular basis helps you activate your right brain more instinctively. Today is all about leaning in to your intuition—listening to that quiet voice inside of you that pushes you to see existence beyond the physical plane.

Many of us can listen to our intuition only when we are still enough to notice and be aware. When we are grounded and still, we have the discernment to distinguish between intuition and the ego. However, over time and with practice, we can build trust within ourselves and become more intuitive even when we're not in the perfect environment to be guided by the Universe. We can move past the resistance of the ego and learn to listen without struggling against it first. Your soul whispers to you and your ego screams—with time, you can learn to focus on that whisper.

I've ignored these whispers at various points in my life. There were times when my soul was telling me to follow my heart, but my beliefs were so calcified that I was not living in alignment. If you feel imbalanced in this way, sit in silence and ask yourself what you need. You may find that when you open yourself up to your soul or your higher self, the whispers will be too loud to ignore. You may find that you need to make a change in your life, but your ego was just too afraid. Let yourself feel that these fears were valid: change can be difficult and scary, and it's possible that before you can make that change, a lot of internal shifting will need to happen beforehand.

Listening to your intuition will help you to discern when to take action and when to rest. Tuning in to your intuition will also help you to know where your energy is—whether your energy is in the "chasing" mode or "attracting" mode. When you launch a desire, when you set an intention, you'll want to be magnetic and not repellant. Remember that when you chase, you push the thing you want farther away from you. Instead, focus your attention on it but don't become obsessive and fixated, because your energy will just project your lack of that thing. As like attracts like, the Universe will only deliver that which you are. Feel the energy of the thing you want and you'll see where there is stagnancy and where energy is flowing. Use the practices below to develop your intuitive abilities and learn how to perceive—it's such an important sense to develop as you move forward in this journey.

These are some ways you can identify your intuitive gifts. These are metaphysical sensations as a reaction to something that is nonphysical. Some people might have a strong sense of their clairsentience but not as developed in their clairaudience, for example. See for yourself which clairs are prominent for you right now and how developing these gifts can help you.

Clairvoyance (clear-seeing). You can see visions, orbs, auras, and light that are beyond this physical realm.

Clairaudience (clear-hearing). You can hear the subtle realms. You get "downloads" from your spirit guides through them speaking to you directly.

Claircognizance (clear-knowing). You just know. You don't know how you know, but you just do. You have a deep knowing within you.

Clairsentience (clear-feeling). You feel energy from people and spaces. I know many people who don't consider themselves to be spiritual per se say things like "the vibe was off" or "the energy in this room is bad." I believe that most of us are clairsentient.

Clairalience (clear-smelling). You can smell specific odors that are not physically present to you. I know someone who is a medium. She can communicate with souls who have transitioned to the other side. She can smell certain things that were specific to that person.

Clairgustance (clear-tasting). You can taste things that you're not currently chewing or eating or have not recently been chewing or eating. Some people are very sensitive tasters, and this skill might be beneficial to connect to the subtle realms.

Developing Intuition through the Third Eye Chakra

The center of your intuition is the third eye: the Ajna Chakra. Here are some practices to activate your ajna:

Bhramari Pranayam (Humming Bee Breath)

1. Sit in a comfortable meditation pose, preferably with your legs crossed on the floor.
2. Close your eyes and relax the whole body.
3. Bring both hands to your face and gently allow the middle and ring fingers to cover your eyes, and your index fingers to fall on your brows. Your pinky fingers will fall just below your cheekbones, and your thumbs will press on your ears without inserting into them.
4. Bring your awareness to the center of your head, the point between your brows, your ajna or third eye.
5. Inhale through the nose.
6. Exhale slowly and in a controlled manner while making a deep, steady humming sound like a bee. The humming should be the duration of the exhalation.
7. Do this for at least two minutes.

This practice will relieve tension in your head and work to open up the ajna chakra.

Chant for Activating the Ajna Chakra

1. Sit in a comfortable meditation pose. Relax your body.
2. Take three deep breaths to bring yourself to your interior awareness.
3. On your next exhale, chant *aum* slowly pronouncing each syllable a-u-m.
4. Chant *aum* three times and afterward, sit in stillness and notice the vibration you have created.

Asana for the Third Eye

To develop the properties of the third eye, try assuming Balasana (Baal-asa-nah), or Child's Pose.

1. Come to your hands and knees on the floor or mat.
2. Sit on your heels and spread your knees shoulder-width apart. Keep the tops of your feet on the floor and your big toes touching.
3. Exhale and bend forward, placing your forehead on the floor or mat. Bring your belly to rest between your thighs. Relax your shoulders and jaw, and close your eyes if you like. If it's uncomfortable to put your head on the floor, you can use a block or a towel.
4. Stretch out your arms in front of you with your palms facing on the floor. Or bring your arms back alongside your thighs with your palms facing up.
5. Keep your neck in a neutral position.
6. Bring awareness to your third eye and take deep inhalations and exhalations.
7. Stay here for thirty seconds to three minutes.
8. When you are ready to come out of the pose, take a long, deep inhale, and on the exhale, bring your head up, stretching your back.
9. Straighten your legs and lie down on the floor on your back and relax.

Contraindications

Don't do Balasana if you have a knee injury. If you're pregnant, don't press your stomach on your knees. If you feel any pain, gently come out of the pose.

Benefits

Balasana stretches your back, hips, and thighs and helps you activate your third eye.

GO DEEPER

Intuition Exercise

If you can get on a phone call, Zoom, or meet in person, that's optimal, because you're going to need a buddy. I do this with my students to sharpen their intuition skills. The basic aim is to learn how to become sensitive to someone's energy without touching them.

First, ask for consent and pair up with a partner you trust. Then assign who gets to "read" first, and who will be the receiver. I would suggest you be the reader first since you are practicing your intuitive skills. Then, if your partner is interested, you can switch. You're going to begin by sitting in front of each other. Ask your buddy to be as open and as comfortable as they can be, because for you to have access, they will need to open up their energy field.

Both of you should begin with closed eyes. Take a deep inhale through the nose and exhale through the mouth. Make sure both of you are grounded. You can direct your partner by saying, "Open your energies." This simply means that they should expand their energetic field and try not to close it off. It's okay for your partner to be thinking about things. Now tune in. Become still. Relax your body. Focus on your third eye. Listen and feel. When you are ready to come out of this state, direct your partner to slowly open their eyes. If you don't feel anything, it's completely okay. It takes practice. But if you do feel, hear, see, or know anything, report back to your partner.

DAY 31
Yin and Yang

*"Once we achieve this balance, we will see everyone as a
balance of masculine and feminine. Everyone has a role.
Every energy is of equal value."*
—Reena Kumarasingham, *The Magdalene Lineage:
Past Life Journeys into the Sacred Feminine Mysteries*

MASCULINE AND FEMININE is not about gender, but the energies
that are within all of us. Energy is nonbinary, but our current vocabulary
and understanding of polarity and duality are limited to these words. So
for the purposes of the language we currently have to work with, I will be
talking about masculine and feminine energies. In Chinese philosophy
they are referred to as *yin* and *yang*. In astrology, they are the lunar and
solar, and in the chakra system, the ida and the pingala.

In the Law of Sexual Energies from the Universal Laws, you were introduced to the Divine Feminine (yin), which is space, darkness, chaos, softness, passivity, potential energy, age, infinity, and your subconscious
mind. Like energy, the Divine Feminine is the foundation of all creation.

It is Spirit—it comes in form and out of form and then cycles again. The Divine Feminine is the "is-ness" or the "being" of all things.

In the West we were taught that when you want something, you go out and get it. That cause and effect is expressed through yang: masculine energy. But as we've learned, there is a time and place for taking action, and also a time in which the opposite is true. Yin is taking care of your mind, heart, body, and soul and preparing them to be the vessel that attracts the things to you. Systems and structure are masculine, but the feminine is flow. Notice how the concepts of "cash flow" and "income stream" have yin energies and associations? Yin is also aligned with the element of water, as well as the sacral chakra—to be in yin is to be ready to receive the essence of our desires.

But yin doesn't just mean you wish on a star and do nothing. It doesn't just mean resting, either. It's consciously allowing things to flow to you. It requires you to be sensitive to other sensations beyond your five senses—to listen to your intuition. Yesterday you listened to your clairs and spent time noticing the shifts in the environment around you. Yin means observing and having awareness of the actions of others so that when the opportunity comes, you're ready.

Your manifestations come through when you are in this state. When you are rested, nourished, and loved, and when you have enough energy, you are ready to attract what you desire. What are you magnetizing through your energy?

We are often taught to believe that more is better, that quicker is better, and that you have to work hard to get what you want. But so many of us have—rightly—begun to question this paradigm. After all, if working harder were the answer, then a lot more people would be rich. But they're not. There is a Zen Buddhist saying: "Before enlightenment, chop wood and carry water." You manifest when you take your focus off the big picture, or the big dream, and give yourself to your everyday, mundane tasks, when you take in the lusciousness of each moment and just experience what you are doing. That's the most important step in manifestation:

detachment. Allow nature to take its course. When you focus too much on the thing you're manifesting and why it's taking so long, you are micromanaging the Universe. With love and peace, stop that. When you do that, you're basically telling the Universe that you don't trust it.

I'm specifically calling your attention to the Divine Feminine because, chances are, if you live in a modern Western place, you are familiar with the masculine, possibly the wounded masculine. The wounded masculine may exhibit behaviors such as control, aggression, violence, and abuse of power. Maybe you're more comfortable with working and doing but not as familiar with the feminine energy of waiting, contemplating, and receiving. There has to be an equal balance of feminine and masculine energy at all times and the discernment to know when to *be* versus *do*.

Chop wood, carry water. Today, stop worrying about getting the thing you want. Clean your bathroom. Buy groceries. Open your mail. Do the things that must be done. Take this time while you're "waiting" for your manifestation to arrive by living your life. Living in the moment puts you in the receptive mode and, if the proper detachment is achieved, paradoxically you will be ready for the next steps in the days to come.

Alternate Nostril Breathing

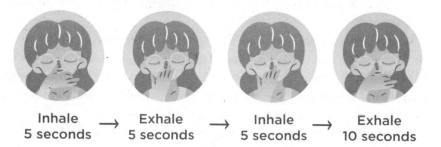

Inhale 5 seconds → Exhale 5 seconds → Inhale 5 seconds → Exhale 10 seconds

Sit on the floor in a crossed-legged position. Feel your sit bones rooted down to the floor as the crown of the head is reaching for the heart of the sky. Place your hands gently on your knees or in your lap. Close your eyes. Relax. Feel the spaciousness of the present moment. Take a deep inhale through the nose, hold for four seconds, and exhale out through the mouth. With your right hand, tuck your index, middle, and ring fingers in with your thumb and pinky out. You will place your right thumb on your right nostril. Inhale through the left nostril for four counts, hold for four counts, then close the left nostril with your pinky finger and lift the thumb and exhale out the right nostril for four counts. Hold for four counts. Repeat, alternating nostrils. If you are left-hand dominant, use the left hand, left thumb, and left pinky.

GO DEEPER

Wu Wei is one of Taoism's most important concepts, which is translated to mean "non-action" or "non-doing." To our Western minds, it might seem nonsensical to do nothing, especially when our lives are so busy and full of needs. However, Wu Wei is about being in the flow state. To be in Wu Wei is to cultivate a state of being that's in alignment with the ebb and flow of nature's cycles. Today, research Wu Wei, or just put it into practice by taking a day off to do "nothing." Be in nature, and simply observe. What a wild idea.

DAY 32
Finding Your Soul Family

"You are the average of the five people

you spend the most time with."
—Jim Rohn

MY FIRST FORAY into taking a manifestation course was in 2018. The manifestation coach told us to find "expanders"—in other words, people who looked like us who were doing what we wanted to do. The women of color in the group brought it to the teacher's attention that for marginalized groups, it's not that simple. Many of them spoke up about their need to manifest for survival, not just to improve their life or follow their pleasures. Also, they pointed out that the lack of representation in finding these "expanders" was a major problem. When there are so few people who look like you and are also doing what you want to be doing, what is the solution? Instead of listening to these issues and responding thoughtfully, the teacher kicked us all out of the group. In short, my first experience with a manifestation course was not positive—but I did learn a lot. First, it taught me what not to do as a leader. Second, I believe that experience helped me to prepare to write this book. Since that incident, our cultural climate has definitely improved, but it's not nearly where it needs to be—we need to be able to acknowledge and discuss the systemic issues that prevent us from using tools to manifest our realities. What if no one in your family or lineage lived out their dreams? What if you were taught to believe that your dreams are impossible? We need to be up front about the very real problems that we are facing, and we need community to do that.

With time and effort, I was able to find my people: the people who inspire me, and not just celebrities or influencers. When I started traveling full time in 2017, I met other women of color who were entrepreneurs, healers, artists, and community builders. They were also advocates and activists helping BIPOC, LGBTQIA+, disabled, and other marginalized groups.

During this time, I did a Marie Kondo'ing of my friendships. I looked around at my circle of friends and took note of whom I felt comfortable sharing my dreams with. I wanted to be able to be completely honest with them about my goals and plans, without fear of judgment. If there were people who did not support me, I let those relationships go.

I'm not telling you to ditch your friends. But today, be honest with yourself about the people around you. If you don't feel supported by your friends, know that you can definitely make new ones. Call in the energy that you want to experience. You should be around people who you admire, who are smarter than you, who have talents that you find amazing, who seem to have unending bravery and strength. When you are around people you respect and look up to, you will rise to the occasion simply by osmosis. And when you need a support system to hype you up and back you up when the going gets tough, you will have the best you can possibly imagine. It's so important to surround yourself with growth-minded people who hold you accountable for your dreams—people who believe in you, who don't take your shit, and who will keep pushing you forward.

When your manifestations start coming together and you start becoming the version of you that you've been calling in, you will rise above. In the process, you may even leave some people behind. Your friends might become jealous of your success. This happens. Just remember that energies are adaptable to change. Accept that to become the person you want to be, you'll have to go where your energy wants to go.

This might trigger some jealousy or discomfort in others. Seeing you make changes may remind them that they are not following their own dreams. Their reaction has nothing to do with you. Instead of trying to make these people comfortable, build your own confidence and set boundaries to find friends who are comfortable with your success, support you, and encourage you. And don't forget to apply the same logic to yourself! The moment you feel an internal trigger of jealousy, ask yourself, "What are these feelings reflecting back to me that I myself want to experience?"

Take this time not just to evaluate the relationships you already have, but to think about how to develop new ones. It's so important not to feel isolated and alone: people need others, and the lack of strong relationships can cause us to turn inward and embrace negative, self-destructive patterns of behavior. As the African proverb goes, "The child who is not embraced by the village will burn it down to feel its warmth." Hurt people hurt people—when we don't feel connection, we experience separation. Isolation is detrimental to our health and spirit, which is why the pandemic has been a catastrophic event on many levels. During the pandemic, I wasn't able to see my friends and family in person as much, but because of technology, I've been able to meet people all over the world. Thanks to my Aquarius placements, I turned to social media and technology as a means to connect. In 2020, I started holding moon circles, as well as teaching online, and in 2021, I started a podcast with a dear friend. Without this community and support, I don't know if I would've gotten through a lot of those times of uncertainty. Consider what you could do to reach out to others both in-person and online. How can you connect with your people—your soul family?

I found soul family by doing things that I was interested in. In 2020, I became serious about learning astrology, so I started taking astrology classes and met a few friends through various astrology channels. I joined a cacao circle and met a whole bunch of lifelong friends there. I started Reiki circles with my students to give Reiki to people on a sliding scale.

We donate the proceeds to charity. Our intention was to spread more love and healing to the world. Because all of us were meeting during a global pandemic, there wasn't time for surface-level conversations. We got deep really quickly. I not only created community, but I became a part of others through mutual interests.

If you are calling in soul family, start by doing the things you love. By doing what excites you, you are inevitably going to meet heart-minded souls. Also, when you do things you love, that energy radiates out and you attract the people who are meant to find you, who make you feel safe, and, like you, can participate in the mutual give-and-take of energies that a true relationship should be. We manifest from our feelings, so it's important for you to feel safe. Take this opportunity to surround yourself with people who make you feel as if you are in a safe space in which you can be vulnerable. When you don't have to perform and wear masks, you can be completely yourself, in harmony and balance with the world around you.

Relationship Audit

List all of your closest friends, particularly those in your inner circle, and meditate on whether those relationships are reciprocal.

GO DEEPER

Maybe one of the things you are manifesting is your soul family. Make a list of qualities and energies you want to surround yourself with. Read the book *The 5 Love Languages* by Gary Chapman—it's an excellent resource for figuring out what kinds of energies work best together.

DAY 33
Healing Your Scarcity Mentality

"If the thought of lack—whether it be money, recognition, or love—has become part of who you think you are, you will always experience lack rather than acknowledge the good that is already in your life, all you see is lack. Acknowledging the good that is already in your life is the foundation for all abundance."
—Eckhart Tolle, *A New Earth*

MOST OF US who start on the manifestation journey begin because we want something that we feel that we don't have. In essence, we start manifesting from a place of lack. But the Universe doesn't care about what you want: it reacts to vibration, so if you are manifesting from a place of lack, it will keep giving you the same vibration you currently have until you change it. If you are in a state of wanting, you are resisting, because you are noticing what you don't have. The whole point of manifesting is to release resistance and be in the receptive energy that we discussed on Day 31. When you notice yourself focusing on what you don't have, remember to refocus your attention and energy back to the things you do have.

You can train your mind to see a world of abundance versus lack. For those of us who have seen this world with a lens of scarcity all of our lives, this process will take time. I'm going to use the example of money, because it's the thing that most people want to manifest. I'm sure you've heard many times that money is energy—I've mentioned it myself earlier in this journey. Money is used as an exchange for a good or service. It was meant to be just that until we associated it with other things like power, safety, and security. We have attached meaning to money even though money is neutral. Money has been represented in various physical forms over time. During ancient civilization, salt and grain were used as forms of exchange. Then it was gold, bank notes, dollars, and now digital currency. Money is going to be more and more elusive to us as it is exchanged through our technology versus our hands.

I've always heard this, even through my church days: that God gives you everything that you need. So then, why did I always feel *without*? I felt that I was without money, without recognition, without love, in spite of that teaching. So how do I shift my mindset and feel that I *have*? Whenever I feel the strong pull of lack governing my mind, I go for a walk in nature and I repeat out loud all of the things I see. I begin by saying, "I am grateful that I can see, hear, touch, and smell." Start with small observations to shift your focus to abundance in a world that tries to convince you that there's not enough. What do you see? What are you grateful for?

I believe one of the biggest diseases in the world is our belief in lack—it has created such division and separation. It has catalyzed wars, colonization, and suffering. The ideology behind it all is lack. Lack leads to justification in taking wealth and resources from other lands. And while you might not literally practice the ethos behind colonization in your everyday lives, you might manifest it in other ways. The energy of lack and lead to feeling jealous of someone's success, MLM schemes, sketchy marketing, and even road rage—it means blinding yourself to the suffering of others in order to increase your own feeling of security.

One morning, my editor contacted me and let me know that there would be other manifestation-related books launching at about the same time this one would be released. The first words to appear in the email were "not to freak you out." If this was a couple of years ago, I would've freaked out. My ego would've said, "Who are you to write a book about manifestation? There are MILLIONS of manifestation books out there!" But my reaction was different this time. I truly believe in what I'm writing here, and in the journey we are taking together. I believe that we live in an abundant Universe. Each book you will read has a unique perspective based on the experiences, wisdom, and knowledge of its author, and the more content out there about this topic, the better. We should be filling the minds and hearts of people with inspirational content. My belief in abundance is so strong that I know there is enough for everyone.

When your mind is trapped in a scarcity mentality, you believe that the world cannot provide for us all. Don't blame yourself—so many of us have been taught from a very young age that there is only one seat at the table, and that we must fight for it. We've been taught that there is an apex to the pyramid of human existence and that only a few people may experience complete success. The symbology of this outdated paradigm appears everywhere, even on the dollar bill. In the past, I have felt like I'm in between worlds when I try to reconcile my innately collectivist and community-based Korean culture and my American upbringing, which is more individualistic. But I have come to believe in individual success that doesn't come at the expense of community care and shared resources.

We were taught to believe in lack; we can unlearn it. I will refer back to what we learned on Day 12 here, because when you observe nature, you understand that everything has a season and a time. In the winter, it might seem like everything is dead, but in reality everything is very much alive. It's just that winter is a time of rest and dormancy—and that is part of abundance, too.

In Lynne Twist's book *The Soul of Money*, she writes, "Sufficiency as a way of being offers us enormous personal freedom and possibility . . . the truth of sufficiency asserts that there is enough for everyone. Knowing that there is enough inspires sharing, collaboration and contribution." I believe that BIPOC people have been led to feel that we are the minority and that some of our countries of origin are poor. I've experienced quite the opposite. This is something that I alluded to in the introduction. I am a history nerd. I love learning about why things are the way they are now, and in order for us to understand why things are the way that they are, we have to look back at history.

I co-host a podcast called *The Werk*, and one of our guests, Milagros Phillips, is a race healer who teaches programs that combine historical references, science, research, and storytelling to create compelling and life-transforming experiences. During our interview, Milagros shared that all of the countries at the equator experience abundance all the time because of the temperate weather—they have food all year round. Most of these countries, for example, Haiti, were the richest countries in the world until colonization. Colonizers drained these countries of their natural resources—minerals, crops, as well as money—and then convinced the people who lived there that they were poor.

I've mentioned that colonization represents lack, because colonized countries' existence is predicated on a belief in lack. These places often don't live in lack. They are some of the most abundant in culture, music, food, spiritual practices, and wisdom. But the belief in lack imposed upon them by the empire that absorbed them perpetuates throughout generations—that they are uncivilized or lack the discipline or efficiency of the colonizer. But all it takes to break this cycle is first, to be aware and second, to change the pattern. The truth sets you free.

You change generational patterns by breaking the cycle and halting the repetition of one pattern by introducing a new one. I believe that each and every one of us who decided to show up to the school that is Earth is a potential chain breaker of toxic patterns from our ancestors.

When I asked my sister what she was manifesting for Christmas, she said, "more money." In response, I asked her, "What does money represent for you?" to which she said, "Safety." I asked her how much money she would need to feel safe. She said she had enough, so she wasn't sure why she needed more. That is where the work is. That's looking at your shadow self to know why you don't feel safe and figuring out what needs healing. Simply manifesting more money will not help you feel any more safe or abundant. To be able to feel safe and secure, you must first heal your belief in lack.

Some of you reading this book are manifesting because you are not happy with your current circumstances. Otherwise, what would motivate you to want something different for your life? If you're in a mindset where you feel stagnant or depressed, you won't notice the miracles all around you. When you're focused on all the lack, it's like a veil that covers all of the creativity and prosperity around you.

Apocalypse in ancient Greek translates to "lifting of the veil," and for some of us 2020 felt like an apocalypse on many levels. But it might have also been when you were able to finally see beyond the veil. When you are going through impossibly difficult times and feel like everything is lost and there is nothing to look forward to, it's paradoxically the perfect time to look within yourself and find abundance. When you have to search for what makes you grateful, it's the perfect time to know that it comes from you.

Meditation to Heal Scarcity Mindset

Find a quiet place. Sit on the floor or on a chair. Feel your root chakra being grounded to the earth and the crown of your head rooting up to the sky. Relax your forehead. Allow your tongue to rest in your mouth. Relax all the muscles in your body. Be here in the present moment. Tune in to your thoughts, beliefs, and feelings. Try not to judge what comes through and ask yourself, "Am I manifesting from a place of lack?" Awareness is key. What do you feel like you're lacking? Look at what you're manifesting and ask yourself, "What will this bring to my life? How can I fill that void now with the resources I have?"

GO DEEPER

Write yourself a check just like Jim Carrey did. Write an amount that you're manifesting. For example, Jim Carrey wrote himself a $10 million dollar check for services rendered, and he gave himself five years to manifest it. He looked at the check every day until the date that he'd written came about. On that day, he said that the check started to disintegrate in his wallet. And, in fact, he no longer needed it: he had manifested the $10 million exactly five years to the day for his role in the movie *Dumb and Dumber*.

DAY 34
Cultivating an Abundance Mindset

"Abundance is about being rich, with or without money."
—Suze Orman

I REALLY BELIEVE in the power of aligning your intentions with your highest timeline. Of course it's great to dream as big as you can—we've explored that since the early days of this journey. But it's also a good idea to create a vision that aligns with your values, because when you manifest without taking the time to do that, you may realize that the result doesn't actually make you any happier or satisfied than you already were. For example, many of you may be manifesting a high-paying job. If you get that job, will it make you feel safe, secure, and joyful? Will it make you feel supported? If you set your intentions on the things that are aligned to your highest timeline—that are representative of your values, morals, and soul's mission—then you'll find that your manifestations will be more likely to satisfy you in a holistic, abundant way.

Manifestation based on abundance leads to creativity, love, reciprocal intimate relationships, and generative opportunities that will bring you to joy. Getting to them will require of you to really look at what you value. You will only know this by truly knowing yourself. Manifesting the life of your dreams is about expressing who you really are and feeling whole within yourself. Today is about feeling whole and abundant, in spite of the material circumstances of your day-to-day world.

It is our human birthright to want material things. After all, we came into this world having a human physical experience. I am also advising you to want those things, but to not become too attached to them. Why try to manifest money and physical things when they aren't what you ultimately desire? When your goal is money, you'll never have enough. A stack of bills will bring you a temporary hit of pleasure, but inevitably, that feeling disappears. When you feel whole and complete already, you are magnetic, and wealth of all kinds comes to you. Money, an extremely hot person who wants to date you, a really nice car: all are great on their own, but all are limited resources. Physical money is just a thing. A nice car is fun but will break down. It's fun to date a hot person, but what if they don't support and celebrate you or make you feel excited about the world? As they say, a person cannot complete you. You can, however, work on yourself.

When I worked at a corporate job, I was making six figures and had top-tier health insurance, a 401(k), and all of the financial security I could've ever wanted. But because I wasn't aligned to my soul's calling, it never felt like enough. I experienced an incessant feeling of dread and lethargy. And so, I finally decided to quit that job, because I knew that even if they offered me a million dollars to stay, no amount of money would make me happy.

Money isn't everything. It plays a huge role, obviously, and you shouldn't blame yourself for wanting to see a full bank account or to have the ability to buy that coat you really want. If you're worried about bills, it will be difficult to stop thinking about manifesting the money to pay them. But remember that money is a man-made concept. It dates back to the establishment of the first cities in Mesopotamia around 3000 BCE, when representative money became a more efficient form of exchange than grain, which is how people previously paid for goods and services. With the advent of representative money, farmers switched to depositing their grain in the temple, where they would receive a receipt in the form of a clay token that they could then use to pay fees or other debts.

The money that we know today replaced the barter system, gift economies, and so on. So there was always some form of exchange. We don't even print money to represent its worth in gold anymore, so we've become even more detached from its actual value. Money is made of paper. Paper is made from wood. In reality, the actual value of money is less than a couple of cents. And money is the cause of so much worry on a personal and societal level: the catalyzer of mergers and acquisitions, wars between countries, and often pretty much the primary controller of our minds and lives. That is why we have to simultaneously give gratitude to money when it comes to us but not be too attached to it when it leaves. We have to allow it to flow through us like the energy it really is.

This is why I'm leading you on this journey: ultimately, what you are manifesting is becoming an open channel to have an abundance of opportunities and creative ideas, which will help you to create the life that you want. Abundance means truly being in the flow.

The Tower card in tarot tells us that if you build your life on shaky ground, it will inevitably fall apart. That archetypal image is just common sense when it comes to manifestation: you should build on a solid foundation because that means you've already laid the groundwork for your prosperity. Your foundation in this case is your intention. What do you really value? How do you spend your time and money, and how would you like to?

If you say you value your family, do you spend time with them, or are you always prioritizing your work? If you want to manifest a soulmate, think first about whether you are giving enough time and energy to your own self-growth. Are you doing the work of putting yourself out there? The best way to see where you're holding yourself back is to do a nonjudgmental scan for limiting beliefs—the kind that replay in your mind on loop without you even fully noticing them. If you find them, that's where you need to go deeper before you take the next steps.

Finally, ask yourself how you value yourself. Your value is not contingent on what you do or how you make money. The value that you bring to this world is just being you. If you've associated your identity with how you earn money, today is the time to check in with yourself. If you are like me and from a culture that validates prestigious job titles like doctor or lawyer, make sure you are cultivating value within yourself without the need for external validation. There are going to be times throughout your life when you are in awkward in-between phases and don't have a label—maybe you're between jobs, have just broken up with a partner, or don't have a fixed address. When I didn't have a job title and felt like I didn't know what I was doing, it was so easy to think of myself as small and worthless. But those were the times when I manifested the most easily, because I wasn't attached to anything. I was nothing and everything at the same time. My identity was malleable. So if you're in an uncomfortable phase in life and maybe even feel a little lost, take comfort in the fact that you won't have to fight through attachments in the same way as you might have if you felt like you had it all together. Remember, your whole life is a manifestation and a creation of your beliefs about yourself—you're always a work in progress, even if you feel like you've fully manifested your reality and nothing needs to be changed.

As Iyanla Vanzant writes in her book *Acts of Faith*, "Abundance has nothing to do with how much money you have. Abundance is about feeling rich and having rich feelings . . . To understand abundance is to create what you want without fear." We live in a Universe of duality, where giving and receiving are one and the same. Holding on to things too tightly leads to stagnation, and not being able to hold on at all means that you might not be able to truly experience abundance. Both states are rooted in a mindset of scarcity. This is why you see famous celebrities who were once monetarily wealthy lose it all to overspending because their beliefs were rooted in scarcity. You always want to be in the flow so that when you receive, you give back. Don't give without taking—you deserve to appreciate the things you have, and even ask for more. But don't take without giving, because hoarding is another indicator of scarcity no matter how much money you have.

An important thing to ask yourself is "What does an abundant and prosperous life feel like to me?" When I was daydreaming of the day that I could quit my corporate job, I would imagine what it would feel like to wake up when I felt like it, go to a coffee shop in the middle of the day, take a long walk outside. At the time, I was working early in the morning to late at night with my head down, rarely feeling like I could take the time to appreciate my surroundings or even take a moment to just *be*. And while some people who had the same lifestyle seemed unbothered by it, whether because they were animated by ambition or because they just didn't have the same needs I did, I realized at the time that spaciousness and leisure are attributes of my abundant life. Abundance and prosperity will mean something differently to everyone, and that doesn't just mean money. It's more than that. This kind of wealth is a feeling and a way of perceiving this world.

In Julia Cameron's *The Artist's Way*, she describes creative blocks by writing, "All too often, we become blocked and blame it on our lack of money. This is *never* an authentic block. The actual block is our feeling of constriction, our sense of powerlessness. Art requires us to empower ourselves with choice. At the most basic level, this means choosing to do self-care." Give yourself the space to imagine what abundance looks like to you today, and don't be limited by describing it in monetary or career terms only. Think about the essential qualities of the life you would like to lead, and how you can both give and take from this world without fearing the consequences.

Abundance Journaling

What do you define as an abundant life? Keep track of all the forms of abundance you witness in your Notes app, or by hand in a small notebook. Every time you experience abundance, make sure you take a moment and acknowledge it. Remember: "What you appreciate, appreciates." Here are some things you might add to your list:

- ★ A beautiful sunset
- ★ Coffee from a friend
- ★ A hug from your mom
- ★ Your sister laughing at your jokes
- ★ Your friend saying she loves you
- ★ A beautiful comment on Instagram
- ★ A cute puppy video
- ★ Seeing someone again after a long absence
- ★ Watching a relative recover from illness
- ★ Making amends after a bitter disagreement
- ★ Getting a raise or promotion at work
- ★ Standing up for your beliefs
- ★ A newborn baby
- ★ Vacation
- ★ That feeling after cleaning your space
- ★ An inspiring museum visit
- ★ Completing the entire hike
- ★ Laughing so hard you cry
- ★ Your health
- ★ Mental clarity
- ★ The beautiful flowers and trees
- ★ Fresh air
- ★ Nature
- ★ Wi-Fi and internet access

Don't limit yourself! Everything, big or small, is worth noting in this list. By noticing abundance manifesting itself in the world in both major and minor ways, you are opening yourself up to its energy, and helping your energy flow.

GO DEEPER

This is a core values exercise I did at a Kundalini yoga retreat focused on spiritual entrepreneurship. We were instructed to pick three core values that were important to us, that represented our brand and our business. While it was originally conceived as a business exercise, it's easy to do it for yourself. What are your three most important core values? Authenticity, abundance, alignment? Or something else?

Explore the list of values and beliefs below. Spend time with the words. See which ones resonate with you. Repeat them out loud as you decide which three are the most significant for you.

Abundance	Boldness	Confidence
Achievement	Challenge	Connection
Adventure	Citizenship	Contribution
Altruism	Collaboration	Courage
Ambition	Commitment	Creativity
Authenticity	Communication	Curiosity
Autonomy	Community	Determination
Balance	Compassion	Diversity
Beauty	Competency	Environmentalism

Entrepreneurship	Intuition	Recognition
Equality	Joy	Religion
Fairness	Justice	Reputation
Faith	Kindness	Respect
Fame	Knowledge	Responsibility
Family	Leadership	Risk
Freedom	Learning	Security
Friendship	Legacy	Service
Fun	Love	Spirituality
Grace	Loyalty	Stability
Gratitude	Magic	Success
Growth	Meaningful	Teamwork
Happiness	Work	Tradition
Harmony	Mother Earth	Travel
Health	Motivation	Trust
Home	Nature	Truth
Honesty	Openness	Uniqueness
Hope	Optimism	Vision
Humanity	Patience	Vulnerability
Humor	Play	Wealth
Inclusivity	Peace	Well-being
Influence	Pleasure	Wellness
Independence	Poise	Wholeness
Inner harmony	Popularity	Wisdom
Innovation	Prosperity	
Inspiration	Reciprocity	

DAY 35
Take Inspired Action

*"Take the first step in faith. You don't have to see
the whole staircase, just take the first step."*
—Dr. Martin Luther King Jr.

KNOWLEDGE IS USELESS without application. If you just read this book and don't take any action, then it's just a collection of paper and board—no more effectual than a cookbook, or a book of knock-knock jokes. Manifestation as a concept won't lead you to what you desire. I don't want you to absorb the information without creating real change, so today, take action in whatever way you feel is necessary to create momentum in the journey we are taking toward co-creating your new reality. And, to be clear, action does not always mean what we think it means: action can be yin, and you could interpret that to mean resting and taking care of yourself.

I want to make a note here that manifesting the thing that you want is the first step. But you also need to know how to hold it once it exists. For example, you might be manifesting money, but once you get the money, what action steps will you take in terms of investing your money? Do you budget? Are you planning to ask for advice from professionals on how to manage your money? The manifestation process is not just the act of bringing dreams into reality. To truly close the gap on manifesting, you need a solid, grounded approach to hold this energy. Sometimes, you don't receive what you want because the timing isn't right or you're being protected—that could mean that you didn't have a good plan for what to do with the energy you were calling in. But also remember that sometimes the truth of what you need to do will not be clear to you and can't be prepared for. In that case, you just have to have faith.

Many spiritual teachers I've listened to over the years use the same metaphor: we are all seeds. Some of us are future oak trees, others might be elm, and some of us might not be trees at all but roses. The point is that you are unique. You are coded with potential. It's up to you to decide whether you want to unlock that potential or not. Give yourself enough sunlight, and make sure you are in fertile ground and that you stay nourished and hydrated. Operate based on your core values and bring your awareness to them. Then, one day you see your true self—your chosen reality—sprout from the soil, and you'll know that all of the effort you put in when the growth was underground was worth it.

In 2010, I started a food blog that transitioned into a travel blog and then became a blog about my spiritual journey. I started sharing my stories. I didn't know who I wanted to be, but I wanted to share myself with the world and learn about it at the same time. Then, in 2020, on the weekend of March 11, New York City officially went into lockdown. At the time I felt like my career as a spiritual healer and educator was coming together in an amazing way: I had three months of bookings, doing full moon circles once a month, and I had secured a number of exciting collaborations from brands and companies I supported. Then, it all fell apart. All of the collaborations fell through for obvious reasons. I had to cancel my bookings. I couldn't even hold a full moon circle in person. I would be lying to you if I said I wasn't devasted. I was heartbroken. I had no job prospects lined up, three months of income vanished in an instant, and I moved back into my childhood home to stay with my parents. Overnight, it seemed like I had lost twenty years' worth of momentum.

But I took the time to revisit my old blogs and think about my relationship with social media. I couldn't meet up with people in person, so it was really the only place where I could pursue my core values of sharing information with the world and learning about it in return. This was about the time I started my TikTok account. If you're reading this way into the future and TikTok doesn't exist anymore, it's a social media platform where you can share videos. At the time, you could only upload fifteen-second snippets of video. Before the pandemic, the thought of starting another social media platform overwhelmed me, but at the time I was in need of a creative outlet. To be honest, when I first started it, I just danced. I would practice from a viral dance video all day and then share my take. It felt so good to just move my body and to share something different about myself than what I was used to.

It was around a month in that I started sharing my spiritual practices and perspectives and my videos started going viral. I went from 50 to 75,000 followers in six months. At the time, there weren't as many people sharing content—there were a lot of videos of people dancing and baking bread. But with so many people feeling lost during the pandemic, there was demand for a way to make meaning out of the chaos of the time. I created videos about practices that had helped me find meaning: Reiki healing, meditation, astrology, and manifestation.

I took action based on what I loved and what I wanted to share that felt in alignment with my values. I noticed the kind of content that people were interested in, and I put myself out there and showed up every single day. I share this because TikTok led to so many opportunities that I didn't even see coming. There were so many opportunities that weren't even on my manifestation vision board. How could they have been? I had no idea that a pandemic was coming. When I started that food blog back in 2010, how could I have known that we'd all be stuck at home for three months with nothing to do?

I also didn't dwell on what had happened when I lost so much work in March 2020. I was disappointed, but I didn't let that feeling override the deep feeling of gratitude that I felt during those first three months. I felt grateful that my family and I were together, that I had a roof over my head, and that I was taken care of. I used that time to reevaluate my life. I realized I didn't actually want to move back to the city. I also recognized that I had just copied and pasted the hustle mentality that I had loathed so much during my finance days onto my healing practice. As a result, I was burnt out. The whole reason why I quit my finance job was to be able to make my own schedule and have more freedom, but in the silence of the beginning of the pandemic, I acknowledged that I was feeling overworked again.

Many of the companies that I was originally going to work with before the pandemic no longer exist. And while I didn't start my TikTok and Instagram accounts to manifest a book deal, it happened anyway because I was creating content that felt really good to me. It's how my editor found me, so even though I didn't try to make it happen and didn't even recognize it at the time, the Universe was working her magic to bring in all the right people and opportunities my way.

What we want also wants us too. The energy is always around you, but it comes to us when we are ready. So take a step in the direction of your vision today—but also accept that there are aspects of making your dream into a reality that are beyond your immediate understanding and control.

What Step Will You Take?

Since Day 1, you've been taking daily actions toward your manifestations. That might have meant connecting with your higher self, meditating to come into alignment with your core values, or facing your shadow self. Even just sitting with what you've learned each day is an action: receiving knowledge is an action too.

Today, take one action specific to your manifestation. If you are manifesting money, learn about investing, so that when you get the wealth you are seeking, you can maintain it. If you want to manifest a person, download a dating app and create a profile. Sign up for a speed dating event even if you think it's cheesy, or join a sports team where you can work on your support network (or even meet the love of your life—who knows?). Or, if you check in with yourself and realize that first you need to do more healing, make a plan for how that process will unfold: set up a regular meditation practice, or commit to working with a therapist.

GO DEEPER

Share your dreams, wishes, desires, goals, and what you're manifesting with a person you trust. Ask your friend or family member to meditate or pray with you. I find that when additional people also hold your intention, it amplifies its power. Ask your inner circle, "What are you currently manifesting, and how can I hold space for your dreams?" When you share with people who you trust, they can also help keep you accountable to your dreams. And then when your manifestations start coming in, you will have people to celebrate with you.

Week 6

DAYS 36–40

Allow for Infinite Possibilities

This is it! You've done your part of co-creation, and the rest is up to the Universe. In this week, you'll give thanks and beam love to the Divine for all that has happened and will happen. You will remind yourself that you are divinely protected and guided: thank yourself for all that you have done to create a new and better reality!

DAY 36
Love: The Most Powerful Force in the Universe

"Love is quivering happiness."
—Kahlil Gibran

WE ARE APPROACHING the home stretch! This week is when you hand it over to the Universe. During weeks 1 through 4, you did the "work": your half of the co-creative process. You have begun exploring your inner realms, and I'm so proud of you! Now, it's time to practice the art of surrendering. To start this journey, today, we will talk about love.

What is love? It's hard to define a feeling so expansive and nebulous. Yet, when you feel seen, heard, appreciated, touched, and understood; when you feel wanted and desired; when you feel cared for, free to be yourself—it's easy to understand love.

Agape is a word with definitions including "unconditional love" and "the highest form of love, including charity." Agape can also be described as "the love of God for man and of man for God." We humans have such a limited understanding of what love means because so many of our stories and so much of what we're taught about love defines it in such a narrow way. That type of love comes with conditions.

Unconditional love is what binds everything in the Universe together. It is all-encompassing Source energy. I feel this energy when I'm connecting to God and meditating, or I'm going for a walk in the forest, when I see the sunrise or sunset, when I hear my favorite song, when I see a beautiful flower or a butterfly. Agape love is the highest frequency that we as humans can attune ourselves to: the most expansive energy in the Universe. When we do what we love, when we give to others because we love each other, when we create and manifest something because we want to spread that energy around, I believe that is when we are tapped into this energy and the Universe gives us everything we want and more.

When you love yourself and your life, you become magnetic: Everything and everyone is drawn to your energy. Still, we aren't tuned into this energy all the time, because we are human and we get distracted. You're going to feel ebbs and flows through life when you feel disconnected, which is totally normal and part of the human experience. So when you find yourself in an ebb, remind yourself that it's temporary. That's truly the way to get through life's more challenging times. Take the time to address the disconnection you feel—ask for help from your community and your guides—but ultimately, remember that difficult times will pass. And remember, all humans have free will and the power to change their lives, so it's within your power to reconnect to universal love. Take responsibility for addressing what might be making you feel that way and trust in your ability to find your way back.

Many people who are interested in manifestation are ready for the next big thing in their lives, but get stuck somewhere along the way. A friend of mine said that she understood manifestation on an intellectual level, but also said that changing her behaviors to *feel* it was the hardest part about the process. She was right—that's where the work is. You do have to be able to live your visions, believe in them, and *be* them before they show up in your physical world. And that means loving yourself and loving your dream beyond all other things.

Your mind will continue to deceive you because your eyes don't see the thing you're envisioning. This is where you need to do some pattern-breaking. Interrupt any negative thoughts you may be experiencing as soon as you realize you are thinking them. Counteract them with love. Tune in to your feelings, and do things that bring you joy and pleasure. Stop, breathe, close your eyes, place your hands on your heart, and ask yourself, "Does this bring me joy?" Be honest with yourself and only do things and think thoughts that bring joy. Obviously, you're going to have to keep doing unpleasant things in your life like paying taxes, laundry, and taking out trash—not everything in life is going to be fun. But when you are tuned into the bigger picture of your dreams and you cut off self-critical thoughts before they develop, you'll find that you can even carry that joy forward and even be happy paying those taxes will all the money that will be rolling in as the result of your successful manifestation.

When you pay for goods and services, especially ones that help you get closer to your dreams, take a moment to be happy that you are helping to employ other people and support them. Give your money a blessing and say a big thank-you to the person you are paying and to the Universe for facilitating the energetic exchange of money.

The way to align with love is to do the things you love and add love to every thing you do—even the stuff that seems boring but necessary. When you take responsibility for co-creating your life with the Universe, you are manifesting every day through your decisions and how you spend your time. So, how many of your tasks throughout the day can you do out of love and passion? Obviously, you'll have to scale: you might not be filled with passion when you do laundry, but try to see it as a part of the whole picture of the life you want to lead. Your life is a moving prayer, a devotion that helps you give thanks for the life you are making for yourself.

Take special care today and place your consciousness in universal love. Even if you have a very normal day in which nothing particularly special happens, keep yourself connected to the concept that every moment is precious. Imagine yourself as a channel for all of the things that are meant for you when you are in the flow of life. And if you make a misstep or mistake, or find yourself frustrated and distracted, be kind to yourself and remember that the very next moment is a blank canvas—an opportunity for you to start over and begin again. Take this opportunity with grace for yourself and your world, because you love your life and you love yourself.

Love in Action

To love your life is to truly live it. Every year, I create a bucket list of things that I want to do. I resolve to do them with or without other people because I won't wait for someone to live my life. However, life is always more fun with friends and family so if you can do this with others, please do! This is a list that I've created, but if there's something that you want to do that's not on there, please put it on the list and do it! You can do one or as many as you want. You can also continue doing them after our forty-day journey together.

1. Go to a new restaurant
2. Try a new cuisine
3. Cook a new recipe
4. Learn a foreign language
5. Go on an adventure
6. Take a dance class
7. Take a road trip
8. Take a photography class
9. Hug a tree
10. Buy yourself flowers
11. Dance in the rain
12. Watch a sunrise
13. Watch a sunset
14. Go to a planetarium
15. Jump on a trampoline
16. Sing karaoke
17. Ride a horse
18. Lie on the grass
19. Have a picnic
20. Attend a live music concert
21. Play in the sprinkler
22. Stargaze
23. Go camping
24. Connect with an old friend
25. Make eye contact with a stranger
26. Volunteer
27. Create a bonfire and don't forget the s'mores!

28. Plant something
29. Go sledding
30. Send snail mail
31. Learn to drive
32. Fall in love
33. Learn an instrument
34. Live abroad
35. Have a long lunch

36. Have a movie marathon
37. Explore your city or town
38. Visit a national park
39. Kiss your crush
40. Write a book

GO DEEPER

✦

Do an act of kindness for a complete stranger.

DAY 37
Gratitude

"When I started counting my blessings,
my whole life turned around."
—Willie Nelson

"THANKS IN ADVANCE." That's a phrase we sometimes use to thank people ahead of time for something they haven't done yet. Try the same phrase on yourself: Give gratitude for your manifestations before they arrive, because it tricks your subconscious mind into thinking that you already have what you're envisioning. It's also a great way to celebrate your wins, both big and small. Don't wait for accolades and promotions to give gratitude—every moment is an excellent chance to celebrate the fact that you're alive. Today is a perfect day for a celebration: Day 37 is about thanking yourself in advance and metaphorically popping the cork for all that you have achieved and will achieve in the future.

There are a number of ways to give gratitude and celebrate that you might want to try out today. One of my favorite ways of expressing my gratitude is to bring offerings to nature, especially when I go to the ocean. I say a few words of thanks and a prayer for my family and friends. I imagine that energy being carried by the waves. I also give gratitude every morning by praying at my altar. I have a photo of my ancestors there and thank them for watching over my family. I revere them and the sacrifices they made for us to be here. Every time I receive money, I thank the person who sent it to me, as well as the Universe. I also thank myself for not giving up. Channel Snoop Dogg's speech when he received a star on the Hollywood walk of fame by saying, "I wanna thank me" and give yourself some love for never taking days off, believing in yourself, never quitting, and giving more than you receive.

What you focus on expands, so instead of focusing on what you lack, focus on what you have. Remember that giving and receiving are one and the same: gratitude is thanking the Universe in advance for your blessing.

Gratitude List

List all of the things and people you are grateful for, and then read your list out loud. Make sure to tell people how you feel about them. Open up your heart, because that energy will expand. Write a letter, call, text, or email someone who you would like to express your gratitude for. Tell them exactly what they mean to you. Don't wait until they're married, get a promotion, or have a birthday to tell them how great they are. Today is your day to do it!

GO DEEPER

Thank your future self and your past self for making this happen, and thank yourself for feeling all that wealth now. Celebrate your manifestation now by throwing yourself a little party. Yes, this is for real! Get some champagne, or if you don't drink, pop some non-alcoholic bubbly. Shake your body and do a celebratory dance, shout out in happiness, eat a piece of cake. Basically, do whatever it is that you do to celebrate because your manifestation is already here!

DAY 38
Detachment

"Close your eyes. Feel it. The light. It's always been there.
It will guide you."
—Maz Kanata, *Episode VII: The Force Awakens*

ON DAY 36 you connected yourself to universal love and spent the day loving yourself and your life. On Day 37 you celebrated and gave gratitude. Now it's time to detach from the outcome: simply sit back and allow the Universe to bring it to you. You can do this by reminding yourself to connect to the essence of your desire as opposed to the form.

There were times when I felt like God or the Universe turned off my ability to manifest. I would stare at my vision board "waiting" and looking at people around my age who I felt were achieving *my* dreams. Fuck divine timing; when was it going to be my turn? Hindsight is 20/20, of course: now I realize I was going through a Saturn Return, a gnarly astrological transit that forces you to reevaluate your life when you turn about twenty-nine years old. However, at the time I felt that my life was falling apart, and I was angry. It sucked, but there is a lesson to be learned here. My anger and frustration forced me to review what I actually valued.

Because I felt that I was getting nowhere, I had to ask myself what feeling I was trying to attain. I realized that when I was manifesting money, what I really wanted was to feel free. When I was trying to bring a soulmate into my life, what I really wanted was to feel desired and loved. I had to take the time to rewire my neural pathways and *feel*—and detachment is a necessary part of that process.

Wanting too hard is a very common misstep, and everyone does it. When you are manifesting a soulmate—a divine counterpart, your lobster!—most people will envision this person by listing physical characteristics, how much money this person makes, religious beliefs, and on and on. In other words, they try to create this person not based on how they themself feel but by what that person *is*: ego-based identifiers and not values that are aligned with their souls. If you're doing this, today is the day to stop. When you focus on yourself and do the work, you will find each other, because you will be drawn together like magnets. What is meant for you will find you.

When we are too attached to form—how something should look—we will not be aware enough to see what's right in front of us. The right person to talk to, the opportunity to kickstart your business, your perfect soulmate: they could be right in front of you, but if you're distracted by a vision that is ego-based, you might not see any of these things or take action to bring them into your life.

Remember on Day 10 when I shared Chris Oh's manifestation story? This is a great example of detachment. Her dream was to live in London, but that wasn't going to happen because international visas and customs were out of her control. When she surrendered, she realized that what she was manifesting was what she was already experiencing in Portugal, her Plan B.

Always remind yourself that you need to focus on the essence—the feeling as opposed to the form. This is the basis of so many rom-coms. You know the story: the protagonist doesn't realize the love of their life was right in front of them all along. Our minds are often the very things that hold us back from "seeing" our manifestations because we are too busy waiting for what we expect. That is why I'm guiding you toward meditations that require you to close your eyes, because it's a step that physically compels you to focus your awareness inward.

I remember watching Oprah share her story about how she manifested her dream role in the movie *The Color Purple*. She was a mega fan of the book. After she auditioned, she didn't hear from the producers for three months. She decided to take matters into her own hands and call the producer directly, which did not go very well. The producer scolded her for calling him. After she hung up, all of her self-limiting beliefs came flooding back to her, and she felt like she had hit rock bottom. She said that she started to cry and sang "I surrender all." She said she did this until she was able to release the role and bless the other actors who had been cast in the movie. But then, miraculously, she received a call from Steven Spielberg himself, and she was offered the role. There are so many stories similar to Oprah's, which to me signifies a pattern in how the universal energies work. The moment you surrender, the resistance releases, and your manifestation comes in.

Instead of asking the Universe, "Is this going to happen?" I invite you to ask instead, "How can I make this happen with what is in my control?" By reframing the question, you are reinforcing the belief within yourself that your life is in your hands, and you have the power to create your life.

Detachment Meditation

Close your eyes. Feel your sit bones rooted down to the chair or floor beneath you. Feel the crown of the head rooting up to the heart of the sky. Feel expansive in your physical body and your energetic body. Allow the release of any tension. Notice where you feel contracted, and let it go with your breath. Inhale through your nose to a count of four and exhale for a count of four. Repeat this for one minute. Bring into focus what you're manifesting right now. Visualize it as if it's happening right now. Conjure up all the images you need to get you there. Again, this is happening now. What does it feel like to have this manifestation into your life now?

GO DEEPER

Go on a walking meditation. I highly recommend walking outside in nature and focusing on the feeling you are trying to cultivate. The essence of your manifestation, *the feeling.*

DAY 39
You Are Divinely Protected

"Trust me, I know what I'm doing."
—The Universe

ONE THING MY ENERGY COACH told me that has stayed with me is that we are always being watched over and guided. Again, that Divine could be a number of forces, depending upon your perspective: God or the Divine Feminine, Source, your higher self, Mother Earth. In any case, something to remember today is that you are not alone in this; you are being guided by the Universe, and you are always being supported.

By extension, you are never given what you are not ready for. That means that if you don't receive your manifestation on your timeline, you are being protected, because either something better is coming along or your timing is not right. When you live this lifestyle in the long term, you'll have experiences that make it hard to deny that there is a loving thread that weaves through everything and everyone. The same intelligence that tells a flower when to bloom and a butterfly to spread its wings is the same one that guides your life. When you feel this massive energy emanating through your heart space or through an act of kindness from another person, it is a reminder for you to acknowledge this magical essence.

Because we are humans, we have a limited perception and can't always see the big picture. We might get glimpses now and then, whether through meditation or a mystical experience, but we human beings tend to process our lives through our past experiences. To counteract that, continually check in with the fact that there's a lot that you just don't know. In addition to everything else we've explored in this journey, the manifestation process is also about building a relationship and trust with the Divine Power you can't always access or experience directly. Trust that it has your best interest at heart and that sometimes manifestations are withheld from you because your higher self is experiencing multiple timelines at once and it may understand more than your conscious mind is capable of understanding. Have you ever experienced a synchronistic event that could have happened only because everything in your life at that time—the people who were there, the place where you were, your state of mind—had to be perfectly aligned for you to experience it? Whenever that happens to me, I get giddy inside, because I know that I'm being guided by the Divine.

You're reaching the end of this journey, and so this is the day to strengthen your belief in this power. But it's also the time to reconcile it with all the other tools at your disposal: your spirit guides, ancestors, and beings from the other realms, but also your free will. Your guides cannot intervene without your asking them for help. Sometimes, the Divine steps in, and unexpected events happen for us that we might not have known we were ready for. Those are the moments in life that set off a chain of events that change your life forever. Possibly for the better, if you choose to see it that way. You created an altar and developed a prayer and meditation practice to build a relationship with the energies that aren't present on the physical plane. Continue to communicate with all these properties, both in your practice and through signs and synchronicities.

Why Not Now?

As we near the end of this journey, you may be feeling frustrated that your manifestations have not begun to show up in the physical world. If they haven't come in yet, ask yourself how you feel. Do you feel abundant? Do you feel whole? Do you feel love? Do you feel rich? If the answer is no to any of those questions, then go deeper. Go back to a previous week or day and start again, not with anger, but with gratitude for the time you are giving yourself and for the divine forces that will be guiding you.

GO DEEPER

Ask your guides to help you see what you don't see. That could be through meditation, but divination tools are also helpful here. For example, when I feel frustrated and blocked, I pull tarot and oracle cards and tune in to the answers I receive.

DAY 40
Faith and Trust

"I find your lack of faith disturbing."
—Darth Vader, *Star Wars*

CONGRATULATIONS—TODAY IS THE last day in our forty-day journey. While manifesting can never be restricted to the schedule of your choosing, because you have spent the time it took to read this book, concentrating your energy and examining your own mental state, you have taken appreciable steps toward co-creating your new reality. Your visions may have started to appear in the physical world, or you have gotten to a place mentally where it feels natural and affirming to act *as if* as they continue to coalesce. The Universe may be furiously sending you signs—or perhaps you've already gotten the thing that was meant for you, even if it doesn't look like what you originally imagined. In any case, today, treat yourself with kindness, and feel the warmth of self-love and hope for the future. And then, my final bit of advice is trust the Universe!

So many of us were taught that if we want something, we have to go out and get it ourselves. The message in school and career is often that we should work hard to get what we want. But the forty days we're spending together is not about hustling to get more money, more love, more success.

By now, you've likely found that the opposite approach can be true. How do you get what you want? So often, that's left up to the unified field of Infinite Intelligence. There's so much that you can't control, and today is about having faith and trust.

The fact of the matter is that your manifestation will most likely happen in a way that you don't expect. If you're expecting it, then you've created it before. You may have been taught to look outside yourself for an answer. You may believe that if you spend enough time seeking, answers exist out there in the world somewhere. We're encouraged to put in the hours, keep our noses to the grindstone, and generally be more in active yang energy. But this is like micromanaging the Universe. Believing that you can roll through your to-do list and, in doing so, control the outcome of your life—that's simply not true. If you're pushing that hard, you don't trust what's meant for you. You are manifesting every moment in your life, and you need to stop right now! This forty-day journey was to get you to a place where you could manifest from a place of wholeness and alignment, and if you're just jumping from day to day asking what the next step is, unfortunately you may be asking the wrong questions.

I am turning forty this year. I can remember when I was eighteen, twenty-one, thirty: I can picture in my mind what it was like to celebrate other milestones. In the same way, during those years I spent plenty of time picturing where I would be by the time I was forty. But now that I'm here, it looks different. So sometimes I'm tempted to account for myself and ask myself, "Did I try hard enough?" Instead, I reprogram my thoughts: I feel blessed at how my life turned out in a way that I didn't expect. I think about all the wonderful people I've met along the way, and the beautiful places I traveled to. I am grateful for all the cool things that I got to do in my forty years that were not even in my realm of possibility at eighteen, twenty-one, or thirty years old.

Your life is a co-creation. You have a partner, and it's the Universe. That means that you give 50 percent of yourself and the other half is up to the Universe. But how do you have a partnership with an entity you don't see? By going through all the lessons we went through up until today. Forty days of connecting to this Higher Power has hopefully given you more information to work with when it comes to your often-silent partner, and more reasons to have faith. You might not be able to sit down and have a coffee with the Universe, or discuss a business plan, but you were able to connect through your spiritual practices, tapping into your intuition, and developing your trust. The goal of manifestation is that you will begin to trust in the timing of your life.

Affirm to the Universe that you are here and have given yourself over to the process of creation. You have detached from the outcome and are ready to step back and let it do its part. In January 2014, I went through the breakup of a long-term relationship and found myself newly single, without a home, without a job, and feeling so lost. I had built a life with my partner, and my dreams were shattered. So I got a tattoo on my left wrist that says *mee-duhm*, which means "faith" in Korean. I got it to remind me that everything happens for a reason. When I find myself in those dark places, I look at my tattoo and I remind myself that I can get through anything. The human spirit is very resilient, more than we give it credit for.

Reaffirm today that you are ready to do the work, both in terms of action and inaction, doing and waiting, giving and receiving. Today is about surrendering the final steps of the process. When I first learned about that concept, I asked all my teachers and healers to define the word *surrender* for me. To me, surrendering felt like not "doing" anything. But surrender is just as challenging and ultimately as rewarding as the more traditional definition of "doing"—you need to develop skills and tools to surrender.

If today—even after you've been contemplating and studying manifestation for more than six weeks—you find yourself falling back to some past beliefs or patterns, that's okay. Just refresh your practices from these past forty days. And if you look around you and you're not manifesting what you want, just remember that this is your ego focusing on your physical reality and pointing out what's not there. Remind yourself that there is more going on than meets the eye. This is so important to remember when you're manifesting. If you don't receive what it is that you desire, (1) it's not the right time, (2) something better is coming, and (3) you subconsciously don't believe it's possible—yet.

Go back to Day 31 and practice receptivity and being in the feminine. Review the practice on Day 4 and connect to a Higher Power. Live your life with gratitude like we did on Day 37. If you did all the practices from the previous weeks, you know that you will have to become the energy you want to manifest, so you've effectively already manifested what you desire. So the last part of this journey comes after you've already done the work; now you give yourself over to forces you can't control.

Divine timing. When I use this phrase with to my clients, many automatically sigh in frustration. I get that. Divine timing can mean one hour or two years—or more. Spirit or the Divine or the higher self that guides the multiple timelines of your life doesn't have a calendar marked with specific dates, or a divine alarm clock. Things happen when they must. And we have our part to do; we must use our free will to not try to intervene beyond the work we've been doing on ourselves. The divine timeline is different than your timeline.

Manifestation requires trust and a radical vision. The root word for *radical* is *root*. It comes from something deep within you. You don't eat the fruit the day you plant the seeds. When you planted those intentions during the first week, trust that there are roots firmly planted into the soil of your subconscious mind. With daily care, watering, and sunshine, they sprout, and eventually a beautiful flower or fruit will come when the timing is right.

Create Art

You are creating an art piece inspired by what you're manifesting for your life. Remind yourself of your visions, intentions, and imagination. Creating a tangible representation of your co-creative abilities will be so rewarding and cathartic.

You can choose any medium that you like. Painting, drawing, charcoal, colored pencils, mixed media, sculpture—the sky's the limit!

Create a sacred space for yourself. Play beautiful music that elevates your mood. You can also use your vision board from Week 1 as inspiration. If you are not used to creating art, you might feel some blocks or thoughts like "This might look bad," and trust me, this is normal; even after taking private art lessons for ten years, I still have doubts about what I'm creating. Try to allow the creativity to flow through you almost as if you're channeling something within you onto your blank canvas. Keep reminding yourself that you're the artist of your life, creating the life of your dreams.

GO DEEPER

Share your experiences and stories with others. When you have the courage to stand in your truth, you encourage others to do the same.

Conclusion

HELLO, BEAUTIFUL SOULS! Thank you so much for trusting me in being your guide throughout this journey. I feel so honored that you've spent your energy and time with me. I really did mean what I wrote about sending you energy the whole time. Before I would begin to write, I would tune in to the unified field and, with the help of my guides, I would ask what you needed to learn, the manifestation stories that would inspire you, and the practices that would help you integrate what you had just learned. Even if some parts of this journey might not have been new information for you, I hope that you've gleaned some new insight about yourself. I hope that I was able to reflect a mirror back to you, to show you how capable you are of manifesting whatever your heart desires.

Acknowledgments

I AM DEEPLY grateful to Kate Zimmermann for taking a chance on me and encouraging me to write this book. Thanks to my parents, Yuna Chung and Ok Young Chung, who, despite worrying about my life choices, have always supported me and my endeavors. To my sister, Sarah Chung, thank you for having always been my grounding force and for always creating a safe cocoon for me and my wildness.

I want to thank me, Laura Chung, for not giving up and settling for less than what I deserve. I also thank my higher self, who is like an eternal flame that needs to be expressed creatively. To my ancestors, who guide and protect me every day. Thank you to the Lenape people and their ancestors, whose land I reside on and where I wrote this book.

I give reverence to my teachers, astrologers, shamans, healers, and cohorts who have guided me on my spiritual journey. Each and every one of you have helped me to peel layers of myself to reveal the truth: Joanna Crespo, Lisa Levine, Sheetal Rajan, Jordan Catherine Pagán, Seo Kelleher, and the teachers at the World Peace Yoga School in Rishikesh, India.

Thanks to my best friend Carrol Chang, who has been with me since we were twelve-year-old girls with big dreams. Also to my dear friends at the

Cacao Laboratory, Federico and Florencia Fridman, for supplying me with cacao, a sacred heart medicine that I drank every day to write this book. To Brittany Simone Anderson for always encouraging me to tell my truth and being a true sister and co-creator. My dear sisters who have brought me back to life: Samantha Caffrey, Niza Disla, and Tanya Grgas.

Thanks to Felicia Cocotzin Ruiz, Chris Oh, Anita Kopacz, and Milagros Phillips for sharing your stories with me and for reminding me that there is power in being a woman of color. That our dreams are not only possible but inevitable. All of the guests who have shared their stories on *Awaken and Align* and *The Werk* podcasts. I felt like I was at wisdom university. I attribute much of my knowledge to hearing your stories.

To my dear moon circle members Natalie Chow, Tina Chaney, Amy Romanowsky, Laura Romero, Sarina Tacovic, Christina Mease, and Venom Spade, thank you for holding space for me when I needed it the most. For allowing me to test-run the manifestation exercises with you. For holding space for my dreams and bearing witness to the power of manifesting. Thank you to all of my clients who have trusted me with their healing journey, there are too many to name here, but you know who you are.

Lastly, I want to thank all of the listeners of the *Awaken and Align* and *The Werk* podcasts, and the communities on my social media platforms: without you, this book would not have been possible. Your words of encouragement have given me the confidence and courage to keep sharing. I wrote this for us and our collective dream of a beautiful future.

Reading List

HERE ARE SOME books that I've referenced in the text—please consider picking them up to enrich your manifestation journey.

Big Magic by Elizabeth Gilbert
Mirror Work by Louise Hay
The Four Agreements by Don Miguel Ruiz
A New Earth by Eckhart Tolle
Think and Grow Rich by Napoleon Hill
The Celestine Prophecy by James Redfield
Acts of Faith by Iyanla Vanzant
Autobiography of a Yogi by Paramahansa Yogananda
The Soul of Money by Lynne Twist
Women Who Run With the Wolves by Clarissa Pinkola Estés
Kundalini Tantra by Swami Satyananda Saraswati
Becoming Supernatural by Joe Dispenza
Synchronicity by Carl Jung
The Alchemist by Paulo Coelho
My Grandmother's Hands by Resmaa Menakem

The Body Keeps the Score by Bessel van der Kolk
The Power of Your Subconscious Mind by Joseph Murphy
Wishes Fulfilled by Dr. Wayne Dyer
The Biology of Belief by Bruce Lipton
Ask and It Is Given by Esther and Jerry Hicks
The Artist's Way by Julia Cameron
Pleasure Activism by Adrienne Maree Brown

About the Author

LAURA CHUNG is a Reiki master, yoga teacher, astrologer, and host of two podcasts, *Awaken and Align* and *The Werk*. She has her Master of Science degree in Industrial and Organizational Psychology. She is an activist and trauma-informed healer who uses her various media platforms to share spiritual wisdom and decolonial education toward collective healing and liberation. Laura uses her intuitive and psychic abilities to help people unlearn harmful programming and remember their soul print, their soul's truth and destiny. Her intention is to help people manifest the life of their dreams.

Social media: @iamlaurachung
Podcasts: *Awaken and Align, The Werk*
Website: Laurakchung.com